Social Complexity in the Making

Social Complexity in the Making is a highly accessible ethnography that explains the history and evolution of Ilahita, an Arapesh-speaking village in the interior Sepik region of northeastern New Guinea. This village, unlike others in the region, expanded at an uncharacteristically fast rate more than a century ago, and has maintained its large size (more than 1,500) and importance nearly until the present day. The fascinating story of how Ilahita became this size and how organizational innovations evolved there to absorb internal pressures for disintegration, bears on a question debated ever since Plato raised it: what does it take for people to live together in harmony?

Anthropologist Donald Tuzin, drawing on nearly three years' field work in the village, studies the reasons behind this unusual settlement growth. He discovers the customs and policies of the Tambaran, the secret men's cult which was the backbone of Ilahita society, and examines the effect of outside influences such as World War II on the village.

This work is a unique example of an anthropological case study which will be widely used by undergraduates and academics. It provides an excellent insight into the ways in which ethnography can contribute to a deeper understanding of what makes a society evolve – or collapse.

Donald Tuzin has authored many works of New Guinea anthropology. He is presently Professor of Anthropology and Curator of Anthropological Archives at the University of California, San Diego.

Social Complexity in the Making

A case study among the Arapesh of New Guinea

Donald Tuzin

London and New York

First published 2001
by Routledge
11 New Fetter Lane, London EC4P 4EE

Simultaneously published in the USA and Canada
by Routledge
29 West 35th Street, New York, NY 10001

Routledge is an imprint of the Taylor & Francis Group

© 2001 Donald Tuzin

Typeset in Goudy by
Keystroke, Jacaranda Lodge, Wolverhampton
Printed and bound in Great Britain by
Biddles Ltd, Guildford and King's Lynn

British Library Cataloguing in Publication Data
A catalogue record for this book is available
from the British Library

Library of Congress Cataloging in Publication Data
Tuzin, Donald F.
  Social complexity in the making : a case study among the Arapesh of New Guinea /
Donald Tuzin.
    p. cm.
  Includes bibliographical references and index.
  1. Arapesh (Papua New Guinea people)—Social conditions. 2. Arapesh (Papua New
Guinea people)—Population.   3. Arapesh (Papua New Guinea people)—Rites and
ceremonies. 4. Social evolution—Papua New Guinea—Ilahita. 5. Ilahita (Papua New
Guinea)—Social life and customs. I. Title.

DU740.42 .T893 2001
306'.089'9912–dc21   00–034479

ISBN 0–415–22899–9 (pbk)
ISBN 0–415–22898–0 (hbk)

Contents

List of illustrations		vii
Preface		ix
1	Introduction	1
2	The setting	19
3	History	38
4	How Ilahita got big	52
5	Residence structures	66
6	The dual organization	78
7	The ritual road to hierarchy	97
8	Conclusion	123
	Notes	131
	Glossary	143
	References	147
	Index	153

Illustrations

Maps

1	Papua New Guinea	20
2	Languages of the Maprik–Wewak area	41
3	Language-culture areas of Ilahita and its environs	59
4	Ilahita village	73

Figures

1	The Ilahita dual organization	82
2	Schematic of Ilahita ward moieties	88
3	Initiation moieties	91
4	Atitapwin's adoption	112
5	Veiled yam competition	116

Tables

1	Ilahita ward populations, 1969	73
2	Ward endogamy rates, 1969	75
3	Ilahita village moieties	86
4	Ilahita ward moieties	89
5	Ilahita initiation moieties and submoieties	108
6	Ritual corporateness of fraternal siblings	110
7	Major sociocultural transitions	125

Plates

	Nggwal Bunafunei spirit house	*frontispiece (hbk only)*
1	The ritual parade	12
2	Women in ritual role reversal	12
3	Man in ritual role reversal	13

4 Shell valuables   13
5 The "voice of the Tambaran"   14
6 Pulverizing sago   26
7 Leaching sago pulp   27
8 Pouring off the rinse water during sago processing   27
9 Trimming the newly harvested short yams   30
10 A heap of short yams ready for feasting   30
11 Luxuriant yam vines   31
12 Bringing long yams home from the garden   32
13 Displaying long yams before a cult feast   32
14 Decorated long yams on display   33
15 Mother and baby   35
16 The Nanu river   39
17 Rice and tinned fish amassed for a feast   47
18 The village court in session   49
19 Young men in a fistfight   50
20 Kotawa frowns at the argument   50
21 Ritual mock aggression   57
22 A man sits ready to greet ritual visitors   57
23 Spirit-house lintel, detail   64
24 Alex Tuzin plays in the rain   69
25 Aerial view of Ililip ward   72
26 A cult elder of the Laongol moiety   85
27 Tambaran statue   92
28 Paintings cover the Nggwal Bunafunei inner sanctum   93
29 The Nggwal Walipeine inner sanctum   95
30 Nggwal Walipeine inner sanctum, detail   96
31 Master artists deal with a construction crisis   105
32 A moment in spirit-house construction   106
33 An aggressive long-yam presentation   118

Preface

Sometimes, major life choices occur as if by accident. I first heard of Ilahita village in the spring of 1968. Since the preceding fall, I had been studying social anthropology at University College, London, with the intention of preparing myself for field research among one of the cattle-keeping peoples of East Africa. In those days – probably still today – the University of London boasted the largest concentration of African specialists in the academic world. To a young outsider like myself, who had not been to Africa, the heat of Africanist interest around London was nearly overwhelming. Not only were there constant offerings of seminars and lectures, but London itself swarmed with academically-connected political exiles and fugitives plotting many of the revolutionary movements going on in Africa in that late-colonial period. So it was only with the idea of enjoying a bit of ethnographic diversion that I enrolled in Phyllis Kaberry's seminar on Melanesia – the "black islands" – a geo-cultural region in the southwest Pacific that includes the Solomon Islands, Vanuatu, New Caledonia, and the great island of New Guinea.

Another reason for taking the seminar was that Dr. Kaberry was my friend. In truth, she was the friend of all students: jolly, nurturing, sociable – our favorite academic aunt. She had grown up in Australia, became an anthropologist there, and, during the 1930s, conducted research on Aboriginal women. From mid-1939 until mid-1940, she worked among the Abelam of the interior Sepik region of northeastern lowland New Guinea, a people now famous among scholars and art connoisseurs for their spectacular paintings, carvings, and spirit houses. Even by New Guinea standards, the Abelam were a fierce people, and it was only with great reluctance that the Australian administration, who had but recently established a local, "pacifying" presence, permitted this young white woman to work alone there. Clearly, they had underestimated her toughness. Kaberry's relations with the Abelam went swimmingly. In the publications arising out of her field work she established the ethnographic importance of this part of the interior Sepik region. She never returned, however. After World War II, having moved to the University of London, her ethnographic interests shifted to the Cameroons, West Africa, where they remained until her death in 1977.

Kaberry's seminar, especially her vivid descriptions of the Abelam, was captivating, and it drove Africa quite out of my mind. By the end of the term I was irrevocably attracted not only to Melanesia, but to the Sepik region of New Guinea. As for recommending a possible field site or potentially worthy focus of study, Phyllis was too far removed from that ethnographic area to be very helpful. Also, recent ethnographic literature on the Sepik was practically non-existent. During the 1930s, a few of the many Sepik groups – the Mountain Arapesh, Mundugumor, Chambri, and Iatmul – were studied by Margaret Mead, Reo Fortune, and Gregory Bateson, and there was some ethnographic coverage dating back to the German colonial period, before World War I. During World War II, however, military aviators confirmed previous inklings that the remote, broad valleys of the central and western highlands of New Guinea were home to huge human populations. Here was a hidden anthropological treasure trove, an ethnographic Shangri-La in which hundreds of thousands of people lived lives culturally untouched by outside civilization. When post-war conditions permitted, research interest flowed there, turning the Sepik region into a neglected, ethnographic backwater.

With one notable exception. Anthony Forge had worked among the Abelam during the late 1950s. Principally attracted by their artistic achievements, Forge had succeeded Kaberry as the ethnographic authority on the Abelam. "Anthony did travel around the Sepik quite a lot while he was there," Phyllis remarked. "Perhaps he would know of a possible field site. He's just nearby, too, at the London School of Economics." I went straight there, hoping he would be in. He was.

Mr. Forge, whom I had never met, received me cordially in his study. Perhaps Phyllis had telephoned ahead, or perhaps my visit came just at the moment he was thinking about research opportunities in the Sepik. Whatever the reason, Forge's response to my inquiry was swift and positive. During the late 1950s, he recalled, with a faraway gaze into the cold London drizzle outside the window, he had once stayed overnight in a remarkable village. It was an Arapesh-speaking village – not Margaret Mead's *Mountain* Arapesh, but a different Arapesh people, the Ilahita Arapesh, whom Mead would not have known about at the time of her field work in the early 1930s. Two features had struck Forge about Ilahita: first, the village's ritual paintings, which were clearly derived from Abelam forms, but which were of sufficient artistry and originality that even the artistically arrogant Abelam deigned to mount them in their spirit houses; and, second, the village's immense size – larger than any settlement Forge had seen, or imagined to exist, in New Guinea.

Intrigued, Forge promised himself that he would return someday to do an extended study of Ilahita. He never forgot the village, but in the ensuing years his ethnographic interests had shifted to the Indonesian island of Bali, and he had lately come to realize that he would not be returning to New Guinea again. Slouchily elegant in the manner of some British academics, Forge tilted back in his chair, squinted through the cigar smoke that would one day take his life, and advised, "Why don't you go to Ilahita and find out what's happening there." That is what I did.

Not immediately, of course. A year and a half was to elapse before I set foot in Ilahita. Preparations were desperately needed: further reading in the Melanesian literature; language tutorials in Arapesh with the late Reo Fortune, then at the University of Cambridge; collaboration with the late Margaret Mead, of the American Museum of Natural History; and removal of my doctoral studies to the Australian National University, Canberra, which was to New Guinea anthropology what the University of London was to African anthropology. In Canberra my doctoral research was supervised with outstanding skill and attentiveness by Derek Freeman, an authority on Samoa and on the Iban of Sarawak. After a couple of months of final preparation, I went to New Guinea, arriving in Ilahita on September 4, 1969. In March, 1970, I took a brief absence from the field in order to get married. My wife Beverly returned with me to Ilahita and was my companion and co-worker for the duration of field work.

The research questions were obvious: how did Ilahita get unusually big, and how did it *stay* big? What kind of New Guinea society permits the large population concentration Forge had beheld? A village of fifteen hundred souls – which is what Ilahita turned out to be – may not seem very impressive. But it is *very* impressive when measured against the fact of the much smaller, often tiny, size of most settlements in New Guinea. Populations of fewer than one hundred are typical, while those having as many as three hundred residents are highly unusual. Doubtless this feature of the social landscape is related to the virtually universal absence of institutions (e.g. formal legal, political, and economic structures) which, in our society, hold residential communities together. Yes, Ilahita *is* impressive – Forge's advice could not have been better – and its very existence evokes a question of unsurpassed and ongoing importance in studies of human society: what does it take for people to live together?

The issue of Ilahita's size is easily stated, the research question easily understood. As events and observations proved, however, the explanation is lengthy and complex, and has thus far occupied three books (Tuzin 1976, 1980, 1997) and a number of articles. The present work uses some ethnographic materials from previous publications – especially from the first two books, which have long been out of print – but repositions them in relation both to general issues of social evolution and, more specifically, to the major transitions undergone by Ilahita that have also occurred in many other times and places in world history.

My Ilahita field work took place in three visits totaling twenty-one months during the period 1969–72 and another eleven months during 1985–6. Major funding for the first period was provided by the Research School of Pacific Studies of the Australian National University, with a supplementary grant-in-aid from the Wenner-Gren Foundation for Anthropological Research. Funding for the return field work was provided by the National Science Foundation. To all these agencies I give thanks for their generous sponsorship.

Ethnographers in the field are dependent on a great many people. In my case it is quite impossible to overstate the contributions others made to my project. At Maprik, the local administrative station, Assistant District Commissioner Mike Neal and Patrol Officer Bob Lachal were especially cooperative in discussing matters of official interest and in allowing me to inspect judicial, census, and other records in their custody. In Ilahita, members of the South Sea Evangelical Mission were always cordial and helpful in allowing me to use their channels for mail and supplies. Among others, I am indebted to Liesbeth Schrader, Ursula Geffke, and Heather Campbell. My greatest gratitude, of course, is owed to the people of Ilahita, who never wavered in their hospitality, generosity, patience, and wonderful companionship. A proper list would be too long, but I cannot refrain from mentioning those whose friendship has been my special privilege to enjoy: Councilor Kunai, Gidion, Supalo, Kwamwi, Moses, Mangas, Ongota, Malalia, Samial, Ribeka, Napaf, Wa'angowa, Akotan, Kwambafum, Soweapo, Behinguf, Ta'ola, and Maufena.

For critical comments on earlier versions of the present work, I am grateful to Guillermo Algaze, Jeffrey Bass, Michael F. Brown, Roy G. D'Andrade, Jacqueline Giordano, Julia Hastings, David K. Jordan, Stephen C. Leavitt, Marc L. Moskowitz, Joel Robbins, Paul Roscoe, Paul Sillitoe Andrew Willford, and D. Brian Woo. My thanks, also, to the technical assistance of Guy Tapper, who prepared the maps and figures, and Adolfo Muniz, who prepared the photographic illustrations.

1   Introduction

From what Anthony Forge had told me, the problem to investigate in Ilahita was plainly two-fold: how did the village become so unusually large, and how did it remain intact? Although these research questions may seem obvious, they were not the sorts of questions social anthropologists working in New Guinea had been asking. Some discussion, it is true, was occurring among area specialists about the limitations of New Guinea settlement size, but the issue was phrased in functional rather than historical or evolutionary terms (e.g. Lepervanche 1967/8; Forge 1972a; Watson 1963). That is to say, their questions were not about how social systems change through time. They were of the type: what combination of environmental factors, cultural values, social structures, or normative practices prevent most New Guinea settlements from growing beyond about 300 inhabitants? My challenge was to discover how a particular village overcame similar restrictions; because, presumably, the village had not *always* been unusually large, the problem presenting itself was at once functionalist and historical. Before introducing Ilahita and the main features of the study, some historical and theoretical background is in order.

Struggling with the past

For much of the first half of the twentieth century, so-called primitive societies were implicitly treated as timeless, unchanging, lacking in history. In part, this was a reaction against the prior excesses of Victorian scholarship, which offered sweeping speculations about humanity's rise, through progressive stages, from Savagery to Civilization (e.g. Tyler 1871; Morgan 1877).[1] The earlier, evolutionist approaches were *universalistic* in that they posited (1) that all humans are comparably endowed with potentials for thought, emotion, and inventiveness – capacities essential to the development of culture; and (2) that the assumed straight-line sequence of cultural advancement is common to all humans, although peoples differ in the distance they have progressed along it. According to that view, primitives living today display not biological inferiority, but an arrested state of moral, social, or technological development. To behold such people, then, is to glimpse our own past; they are our "contemporary ancestors." For scholars interested in the *pre*history of human civilization – the history that preceded written documents – the "time-warp" opportunity afforded by contemporary primitives was the main reason for studying them.

Thus motivated, the activity of collecting information about primitive peoples gathered momentum during the final four decades of the nineteenth century. The more scholars learned about non-Western peoples, however, the more they became interested in them in their own right, independent of the desire to reconstruct our own early beginnings. From this interest, anthropology emerged as an independent scholarly discipline.

With the accumulation of ethnographic knowledge, it became apparent that the idea of universal stages of cultural evolution was inadequate. The fact is, even the most seemingly "primitive" peoples have histories *as long as our own*. Just as our culture is more or less integrated, and more or less adapted to the physical and social environments, so are theirs. If their arrangements are in many (though not all) respects simpler than ours, it is not because they are evolutionarily stunted, but because their adaptation is adequate for survival under the prevailing conditions and has not been noticeably affected by pressures that would cause it to change (Service 1971: 7).

With the realization that non-Western cultures have social integrity and moral coherence all their own, came a shift from universalism to *particularism* in anthropological inquiry; to a recognition that, before it is possible to make reliable pan-human generalizations, it is necessary to understand cultural transformations in their local settings (Boas 1896). How does social system A turn into social system B? If we can't answer that question for some society deep in the Amazonian rainforest, we have no business trying to answer more abstract versions that could be asked of the entire human species.

The problem was, how does one inquire into the local history of a people when that history is unwritten? Historians rely largely on written documents as their lens on the past; what is the equivalent in non-literate settings? Of course, all peoples have *oral* accounts of their past, and these can be helpful. But caution is needed: once events of the past exceed living memory, such representations frequently take on a legendary or even mythic character, making it difficult to regard them as truthful depictions of what actually happened in bygone times. Symbolic analysis can sometimes decipher these accounts in ways that suggest underlying historical realities; but, at best, such exercises produce only plausible speculations.

For the most part, without corroborative evidence the past exists only as a construction of the present – with all the tinkering that implies – rather than as something that can be independently determined. Consequently, it was not long before the call for "local history" became an empty slogan, as anthropologists came increasingly to see their object of study as a culture at a "snapshot" in time: a timeless moment known as the "ethnographic present" – a useful but potentially mischievous concept, in that it seems to admit the reality of history, while actually disregarding or denying it.

In American cultural anthropology, the problem of what to do about history was concealed by the prevalence of studies dealing with Native American peoples. Starting in the middle of the nineteenth century, American scholars urgently undertook to record native customs and languages before they died out altogether, as they were doing at an alarming rate. "History" in that context was equivalent to determining what those cultures were like before being traumatized by White contact. With a few notable exceptions (e.g. Eggan 1937, 1950; Fox 1967) the question of how *that* (pre-Columbian) condition itself came about, was, in practice, inaccessible to inquiry and of secondary importance, though American scholars did continue to profess an interest in history.

In British social anthropology, the neglect of history took a different, more radical turn. Reacting, as well, against the excesses of nineteenth-century speculations about the distant past, British scholars developed an alternative that reflected their different field experiences, which were closely tied to colonial circumstances. Colonial authorities, for the most part, did not seek drastic alterations in the indigenous societies coming under their control. Rather, under a policy known as "Indirect Rule," their mission was to bring order and British law to these regions, functioning as an ultimate authority but interfering as little as possible with customary rulers and practices. The system rarely operated as smoothly as it was supposed to do; but it did enable British ethnographers to observe social traditions that were relatively intact and functioning, not the shattered remnants available to most American researchers, who arrived only after the cavalry had left.

From these circumstances, British anthropology developed an "organic" conception of social systems (e.g. Radcliffe-Brown 1952). Institutions, consisting of clusters of statuses, roles, and conventions, comprised the structures, or "organs" of the social "body." Each was specialized to a particular domain of activity (e.g. economics, politics, religion); the "physiological" counterpart was the functional interactions of the various institutions. Through these interactions, each institution contributed to the maintenance of the body social. A satisfactory analysis consisted of identifying the structures and processes through which a particular society sustained itself in the here and now. Such an analysis is known as "synchronic" ("single-time"), as distinct from "diachronic" analysis, which seeks to understand society as it changes through real time. In its most influential form, the British theoretical position was known as "structural-functionalism."

History, much less *evolutionary* history, had no place in such a scheme; we still did not know how a society moved from A to B. Speculative reconstruction was discredited, oral history was unreliable. Instead, went the view, let the emphasis be on what is more attainable: knowledge of how living societies operate and generalizations about social systems that can be drawn from the world of ethnographic instances. Not only was history methodologically excluded, but with the refinement of its concepts British anthropology came to analyze non-literate societies *as if they had no history*. Not that a certain amount of lip service wasn't given to the merits of evolutionist inquiry. A.R. Radcliffe-Brown, the master theorist of structural-functionalism, in his 1940 presidential address to the Royal Anthropological Institute, conceded that "social evolution is a reality which the social anthropologist should recognize and study" (Radcliffe-Brown 1952: 203). Like organic evolution, he explained, social evolution

can be defined by two features. There has been a process by which, from a small number of forms of social structure, many different forms have arisen in the course of history; that is, there has been a process of diversification. Secondly, throughout this process more complex forms of social structures have developed out of, or replaced, simpler forms.

Just how structural systems are to be classified with reference to their greater or lesser complexity is a problem requiring investigation.

(ibid.)

Unfortunately, neither Radcliffe-Brown nor his students undertook such an investigation. Social evolution remained an eccentric old uncle – living in the past, sometimes humored, but made to spend most of his time in the attic of social anthropology. Thus was anthropological awareness diverted from one of society's most prominent features: incessant change in adaptive response to internal and external contingencies. Only by appreciating these dimensions can we adequately comprehend not merely social dynamics *in the here and now* of Radcliffe-Brown's imagination, but the way in which historical circumstances selectively affect social systems, and do indeed move them from A to B.

Archaeology's challenge

During the height of structural-functionalism's proud indifference to history and evolution (*c.* 1945–70), and despite the persisting scholarly contempt for social-evolutionary inquiry, archaeologists continued their long-standing search for models that would illuminate social transformations in the distant past. Then as now, the major questions concerned the factors that gave rise to pristine early states in the ancient Near East, Egypt, China, South Asia, Mesoamerica, and Peru. Such studies faced formidable practical and conceptual challenges: reliance on the evidence of physical remains, thus favoring materialist and/or ecological explanations to the relative exclusion of ideological factors; and, the need to embrace vast temporal and spatial spans, thus favoring very general characterizations of social-evolutionary sequences and functional relationships. For example, when V. Gordon Childe (1950) spoke of the "Urban Revolution" as marking the emergence of states, or, more abstractly, when Leslie White (1959) spoke of sociocultural complexity arising from the increasingly efficient capture and deployment of energy, one could not disagree so much as shrug in recognition of the unhelpful, tautological truth of the generalization. Such is the fate of most universalistic explanations.

Those notions were a beginning, however. In the succeeding decades archaeology refined its understanding of state formation not only through further field studies, along with technical and conceptual advances of its own, but through increased intellectual collaboration with the relatively few sociocultural anthropologists willing to admit to an interest in evolution. The idea behind this collaboration has been to apply insights drawn from anthropological theory and ethnography to the explanation of changes that occurred in the past: the flesh of the present married to the bones of the past. Kent V. Flannery, for example, combining archaeological findings from Mesoamerica with ideas from social anthropology, interposes between Childe's "Neolithic Revolution" and "Urban Revolution," a "Rank Revolution" (Flannery 1994), thus adding the important element of *ideology* to an otherwise starkly materialist construction of past developments. How and under what conditions do principles of hierarchy develop in "egalitarian" societies that had previously known status distinctions based only on sex and age? This is precisely the sort of question, difficult to answer from the material record alone, that invites collaboration between archaeologists and sociocultural anthropologists.

Similarly, while it is perhaps logical that dense, sedentary populations tend to be associated with substantial food-producing technologies, the precise mechanisms connecting population and subsistence are often not obvious in the archaeological record, but may be illuminated through inferences drawn from the study of living groups. And again, few would deny that population size and societal complexity are functionally related; but this unadorned correlation begs questions of causality, cognition, motivation, agency, and intentionality to which ethnography may have something to contribute. And yet, for reasons just discussed, few ethnographers examine the dynamics of these variables in historical time, in ways that archaeologists might find useful.

The trouble with types

Before suggesting how the story of Ilahita might qualify as instructive in these respects, I must address a prominent theme in studies of social evolution during recent decades, one that has created problems sometimes reminiscent of those of nineteenth-century evolutionism: the adumbration of sociocultural *types* and *typological arrays*, also known as *taxonomies*. Sociocultural types consist of distinctive bundles of functionally interrelated features; they are "ideal" in the sense that they are conceptual constructs which do not suppose that any given society will conform exactly to the type. For example, hunting and gathering subsistence, small local-group sizes, high mobility, kinship-based social organization, an emphasis on sharing among group members – these and other features are typical of band-level societies. The most commonly used typology identifies and distinguishes *bands*, *segmentary societies*,[2] *chiefdoms*, and *states* (BSCS). Depending on the author, different criteria may be emphasized; but, in a nutshell, the sequence ranges from the simplest to the most complex societal types.

Typologies are conceptual scaffoldings that enable us to organize, classify, and compare divers and variable sociocultural phenomena. Without typologies, cross-cultural comparison and generalization would be impossible – or at least very haphazard. For example, in southern Africa a population geneticist, caring about propinquity rather than societal scale, might usefully compare the band-level, hunter-gatherer San with the nearby Swazi, who belong to a kingdom of farmers, pastoralists, and others numbering in the hundreds of thousands. For the sociocultural anthropologist, however, a more fruitful comparison might proceed from the matching of societies of similar scale, such as the San and, say, the band-level hunter-gatherer Inuit of the North American Arctic. Such a matching would allow the investigator to hold a number of shared features "constant" and to concentrate on discovering the causes of specific differences, leading to a more general understanding of so-called band-level societies.

The point of a typology, then, is to reduce the inherent informational "noise" of cross-cultural comparison to manageable proportions. This operation necessarily risks the loss of significant details specific to cases, as well as the categorical exclusion of cases that may be relevant to the analysis. Is the analytic gain worth the sacrifice of this richness? Would a different typology represent relevant, complex realities more accurately and efficiently? Is the typology being granted undeserved explanatory powers? These are the sorts of questions that get addressed to typological procedures. Some archaeologists (e.g. Yoffee 1993) find the typological approach so flawed as to call for its abandonment.[3] And yet, despite its alleged and admitted shortcomings, the BSCS typology has held up remarkably well, and many archaeologists have found it useful (Renfrew and Bahn 1991: 154).[4]

Although, as noted, typological methods are valuable in the service of cross-cultural comparison and in pinpointing important and recurring functional relationships, problems arise when they are applied to questions of social evolution. Considering the archaeological record, can we assume that the BSCS paradigm represents sequential *stages* of historical development from band to segmentary society to chiefdom to state? Certainly not in any automatic or universal sense. As Julian Steward argued (1955) in support of his model of "multilineal evolution," although social complexity obviously proceeds from prior, simpler arrangements, the paths followed in the movement to, say, state-level organization, vary according to local environmental, cultural, and social circumstances. By this reckoning, what supposedly makes the account "evolutionary" is that it tries to explain similarities and differences between instances of a type (e.g. the Incan and Egyptian states) by inferring histories of convergence, divergence, and parallelism from functionalist premises.

Similarly, typologies work fine as tools for describing and classifying diverse phenomena, but they are not so successful in explaining *how* sociocultural forms change over time. This remains a problem even if the *sequencing* of types is granted. It is worth recalling that Charles Darwin was interested in the diversity of living forms not for its own sake, but as a means for discovering the *mechanism* (i.e. Natural Selection) which propels morphological change and adaptive radiation within and across species. If we follow Darwin's original definition of species evolution as "descent with modification," we quickly see that typological approaches, insofar as they do not address mechanisms of transformation, are not evolutionary at all, though by sleight-of-hand they often pretend to be. A common maneuver is to claim or (more often) imply that BSCS is not only a *logical* progression, it is a *causal succession of development*: states supposedly *arise* from chiefdoms, chiefdoms from segmentary societies, segmentary societies from bands. Apart from the fact that actual developments can occur otherwise than in this unilinear fashion (e.g. Flannery 1999; Blanton *et al.*

1999), the approach diverts attention from the true object of evolutionary inquiry, namely, processes of change and the emergence of novelty within sociocultural systems.

Fixating on types makes it very difficult – nay, logically impossible – to conceptualize a group's transformation from one type to another (Marcus and Flannery 1996: 236).[5] By the same token, attention to *transformational mechanisms within social systems* might usefully subvert typological boundaries by revealing that principles of organization common to one type or "stage" of development are present in the preceding stage, though perhaps not in a form that could be readily recognized; nor would such principles necessarily leave material traces in the archaeological record. That is to say, certain defining features of the later stage likely exist as *potentials* at the earlier stage (cf. Flannery 1968: 85; Johnson and Earle 1987: 322). Never mind that collateral changes may be necessary for these potentials to be realized as institutions or ideologies; their presence crucially smears the typological boundary between these adjacent (pseudo-)stages, rendering them counterproductive in the search for mechanisms of change.

To take a more concrete example, one that anticipates the evolutionary flavor of this study, consider the element of *hierarchy* in the ideas and practices of Ilahita. BSCS typologists would have no trouble classifying the societies in this part of New Guinea as "segmentary." Among other criteria, this would include an egalitarian ethos in which sex and age are the main (perhaps *only*) bases for status distinctions; social action would be heavily grounded in relations of kinship and marriage; wealth and power differences would be minor and non-heritable; and political choices would be made by group consensus led by informal leaders known as "big men." The problem is, Ilahita fits almost none of the criteria for a "segmentary" society; indeed, in nearly all respects it is a "chiefdom": a polity – Ilahita village and its tributaries – numbering at least 2,500 persons; politically autonomous entities united under a central authority; pronounced differences of status and rank based on criteria other than age and sex; mandatory levies and redistributions of surplus economic resources; social action based heavily on suprakinship structures; a rudimentary system of hereditary political élites. Indeed, Ilahita is a "chiefdom" in virtually every respect but one: it lacks a chief!

This odd situation is made possible by the fact that principles of "hierarchy" are embodied in forms other than what is normally envisaged in the BSCS model. Specifically, these are ritually constituted hierarchies. First, there is an elaborate cult, known as the Tambaran, to which all males from about the age of 5 belong. Advancement in the cult occurs through a succession of five initiation grades, which amounts to a hierarchy of sumptuary, social, and political entitlements. Although upward movement through the grades occurs as one grows older, the structure of initiation is such that age and ritual rank can be quite out of phase with one another; in any event, cult standing is generally seen by the actors as reflecting not chronological age, but ritual advancement and spiritual excellence. This reckoning extends to the top of the system, which is occupied by the senior-most grade of cult elders: an oligarchy of ritual leaders whose collective political muscle and habits of rule are highly reminiscent of "the chief" found in that other "type" of society.

The rudimentary hereditary élite referred to a moment ago refers to an unusually close-knit subset of cult elders who are master artists. By virtue of the cult's reliance on ritual art and its manufacture, master artists are indispensable and they know it; this condition enables them to exert political authority of a uniquely generalized kind (Tuzin 1980: 194–202). Although the rules of cult advancement would normally prevent master artists, of whom there are about a dozen in the village, from directly transmitting their magic, lore, and technical skills to their sons, a special promotion mechanism enables them to do just that, resulting, *de facto*, in a pattern of hereditary privilege.

The point of this example is not to prove that Ilahita is a "chiefdom" in disguise, or that the flesh-and-blood *person* of the chief is not essential to that typological reckoning. Rather, it is to argue that many of the principles we associate with chiefdoms are *already there* in this "segmentary" society, and that a relatively minor event is perhaps all that would be needed to "promote" Ilahita to the chiefdom "stage" of sociopolitical integration.[6] Were that to happen, retrospective understanding of the transformation would be grossly inadequate if it attended only to the precipitating event – say, a new economic opportunity – and ignored pre-existing social and ideological elements that were already tilting the system in a chiefly direction.

In summary, the genuine study of social *evolution* is not about stringing bands, segmentary societies, chiefdoms, and states as beads on a developmental necklace; it is about discovering the mechanisms at work in the adaptational matrix bounded by space, time, and population; for it is only through those mechanisms that societies move forward, backward, or sideways from A to B. The value of a case study of a particular society, such as the one offered here, is that these mechanisms can be treated at a level of detail sufficient to disclose their workings; such details would be out of place and confusing in a study comparing trait-based societal types. Once established, these mechanisms themselves can become the focus of comparative study – generating, I would predict, typologies of their own.

In recent decades, social anthropology has come to take history very seriously. Owing to the combined effects of the demise of colonialism and intellectual fatigue with notions of structural "timelessness," the anthropological study of society from an *historical* standpoint has attracted a huge scholarly following. At the same time, anthropological interest in questions of social *evolution* continues to suffer from an undeserved equation of evolutionary study with the judgmental nineteenth-century idea of racial or civilizational "progress." Be that as it may, the legacy of earlier scholarship is such that there are very few ethnographic studies which trace the changing historical experiences of a particular society in explicitly evolutionary terms. The present work is an attempt to provide such a study.

Introducing the dual social organization

This book is about the evolving society of Ilahita village and the external events and internal mechanisms implicated in its increasing size and complexity. Over the time span being described, Ilahita society did not change "type," but for reasons just discussed the adaptive, systemic processes that took place during that span are nonetheless entirely "evolutionary" in character. Indeed, one goal of the study is to elucidate the rather severe limits to settlement growth and organizational complexity facing societies of Ilahita's type.

In barest outline: the changes covered in this book began during the third quarter of the nineteenth century, when Ilahita experienced a sudden, dramatic increase in population, along with a radically new threat to its military security. Population without organization spells chaos. One might expect, therefore, that Ilahita's survival as an unusually large village was achieved through a comparably unusual organizational system, with social structures and processes strong and yet flexible enough to bind the expanding community into a unified whole.

Ilahita's integrating system turned out to be of a type known to anthropologists as "dual organization," versions of which are found in many segmentary societies of Melanesia, Australia, Indonesia, and the Americas (Maybury-Lewis and Almagor 1989).[7] The logic of dual organizations could hardly be simpler: the exchange of like for like between pairs of formally opposed social categories. In the great majority of cases, dual organizations function to regulate marriage, that is, they define classes of persons according to mutual marriageability: men of Category A marry women of Category B; men of Category B marry women of Category A. In some instances, the exchanging categories are themselves divided in half, and sometimes those sub-halves are further divided, producing yet more complicated patterns and cycles of marriage exchange. Aboriginal Australians are famous among anthropologists – and *infamous* among their students – for marriage systems displaying this type of mechanical intricacy.

Ilahita's dual organization is not about marriage, though it may have been so in the distant past. Instead, like other dual-organization variants found throughout the Sepik region of New Guinea, Ilahita's system is the framework of the aforementioned secret men's cult known as the Tambaran. Thus, for example, initiation into the five grades of the cult, reaching from early childhood to old age, is administered by the dual organization: Moiety A initiates the sons of Moiety B, and vice versa. These initiations involve a good deal of reciprocal feasting and competition, spilling over into other inter-moiety activities that are not strictly part of cult ceremonialism. In all, the Ilahita dual organization comprises *eight* intersecting moiety systems – or, looked at another way, eight layers of subdivision – making it the most complex system of its type ever documented. An important object of this study is to explain how this organizational complexity was bound up with Ilahita village's success in achieving and sustaining its unusually large size.

The Tambaran: a secret men's cult

The Tambaran is a topic too huge to be tackled in this book (see Tuzin 1980, 1997); but its intimate association with the dual organization makes it impossible to ignore. It is a cult of war and human sacrifice; its magic is designed to protect the village from enemies, quell disturbances in the community, and guarantee the fertility of villagers and the plants and animals upon which they depend. For all these benefits to be realized, women must be rigidly excluded from much of what goes on in the cult. The Tambaran is "what men do," and it is thought that the goodness that flows from masculine ritual acts would be destroyed if contaminated by direct female involvement.[8] Indeed, the first two grades of the cult are intended to wrest young boys and youths from physical and emotional dependency on women, especially their mothers. It is a harsh regime, but in traditional thinking the welfare of the village in all its dimensions absolutely requires it. Variants of the cult exist in virtually all Sepik societies, but few if any carry the misogynistic ("woman-hating") rhetoric to the lengths Ilahita has done.

"Tambaran" is a semantically complex term. The word applies to any and all aspects of Ilahita's central ritual institution. As noted, it refers to the secret men's cult, as a whole. In addition, "Tambaran" may refer to each of the five ranked, initiatory grades of the cult, the spirits venerated in the cult, and the many articles of paraphernalia (carvings, paintings, statuary, flutes, shell effigies, etc.) associated with the cult. Each of these entities has a personal name, as well, but "Tambaran" is the generic term. Moreover, the Tambaran is often personified: its guises, varying according to grade, include animals (mostly birds), an imaginary red-haired dwarf,

Plate 1 The ritual parade of Nggwal Bunafunei initiators. The women in the foreground are dancing backwards, in praise of the men's decorations.

Plate 2 Major Tambaran initiations include ritual gender reversals. Here, two women are shown dancing with spears, something women otherwise never do.

Plate 3 The advent of clothing has facilitated the marking of ritual gender reversals. Here, a young man is wearing a skirt and carrying a netbag on his back, as women do.

Plate 4 Arranging shell rings for ritual display in the Nggwal Bunafunei spirit house. The dagger shown piercing one of the rings is intended to be used to kill a human sacrificial victim.

Plate 5 The "voice of the Tambaran" consists of muffled and enhanced cult songs shouted into these bamboo tubes. The bases of the tubes are placed in large dance drums. While the young initiates perform the song for the first time, their fathers and senior initiation partners provide the human part of the voice. On the right, one initiator bends over to shout the song into the ear of a novice performer.

and an even more imaginary species of gigantic, humanish, people-eating monsters. Over and above these manifestations, the Tambaran has come to be the icon of Tradition: a grand, summary idea that is the personified mystique of a total way of life. Accordingly, traditionalists are sometimes called "Tambaran men," implying that they are emotionally and behaviorally committed to that cultural totality symbolized by the Tambaran. Thus, while the dual organization gives the Tambaran structural coherence and social effectiveness, the Tambaran infuses the dual organization with cultural meaning.

Considering its importance to social and cultural life in Ilahita, my use of the name "Tambaran" to label this institution may seem curious, insofar as it is not a word native to the Arapesh language. It was originally taken from Tolai – a language spoken by a group living far away on the large offshore island of New Britain – which uses it to refer to a category of malevolent spirits. From there, "tambaran" (along with numerous other Tolai words) passed into Melanesian Pidgin (MP), a *lingua franca* that developed early in the colonial period (from the 1880s) as an amalgam of English, German, and indigenous (mostly Tolai) vocabulary items, and simplified Malay grammar. In the ensuing century Melanesian Pidgin spread throughout the land, overlaying New Guinea's immense vernacular diversity.[9] This background does not explain, however, why it is necessary and appropriate to apply a "foreign" label to this Arapesh ritual institution. Allow me to take a moment to do so.

First, "tambaran" has passed over into vernacular usage and is used casually and correctly even by monolingual Ilahitans. This adoption stems from the fact that "tambaran" serves a semantic need not quite met by any indigenous term. It is true that many of the particulars of the cult, such as spirit entities or items of paraphernalia, have specific "personal" names by which they are usually called. But as regards the *totality* of the institution, no Arapesh term has the generic and summarizing character "tambaran" does.

This leads to the second and more significant reason for this usage. From all that I know of it, I am convinced that the Tambaran in this most summary form – as an icon of Tradition, a personified mystique of a total way of life, a champion of cultural identity – *is a creature of the colonial era.* Only upon contacting Europeans and, later, New Guineans from distant parts of the island, did the people of Ilahita encounter radical cultural and racial differences. The experience changed the cosmological landscape for the people of Ilahita; the cognitive need arose to perceive and identify themselves as culturally distinctive. Thus was born, under colonial circumstances, the capitalized, summary notion of Tradition, and the institution of the men's cult was metaphysically upgraded and given the name "Tambaran" to embody this new notion. None of this was conscious, none deliberate; it simply emerged, in the unreflective, intuitive way that symbols generally do.

From its advent in the 1870s (by my estimate), when it was adopted from the neighboring Abelam people, until the abolition of traditional warfare in the early 1950s, the integrative effects of the Tambaran and the dual organization brought great social, diplomatic, and military prosperity to Ilahita. Early in the twentieth century, brief, bloody contact was made with Europeans; in the late 1930s, young men began venturing forth to work short stints on the coastal and island plantations. Thereafter, interactions increased with the outside world of Europeans and other New Guinea peoples; some of those experiences powerfully affected the processes of change going on in the village. With the fateful cessation of endemic warfare (early 1950s), the village entered a "modernizing" period of more intensive contact with external agencies. The Tambaran continued to flourish, but by the mid-1970s it was becoming clear that the days of the old ways were numbered.

In 1975, Papua New Guinea achieved national independence from Australia. The event brought major changes to the local level, in particular, schools, village courts, and a growing assertiveness on the part of women and young people. These and other new elements seriously undermined the power of the traditionalists – the Tambaran men – leading to a Sunday afternoon in 1984, when the men, taking history and culture into their own hands, destroyed their cult by publicly revealing its secrets to the women. To be sure, the Tambaran had been withering on its vine for over ten years; the act of destroying it would have been emotionally and politically unthinkable were it not for the fact that it was almost dead already. Still, revealing the Tambaran's secrets to the women – precipitating the very crisis that the men had privately feared and dreaded for generations – was a profound symbolic deed, and its repercussions were of a width, depth, and length worthy of the majestic institution that the deed had obliterated.

In outline, Ilahita's story can be seen to cover four historical phases, separated and yet linked by punctuating moments largely produced by agencies outside the village system. Bearing in mind, also, that each phase was germinated, in part, from seeds planted in the preceding phase, they are as follows.

- The *Pre-Tambaran* phase refers to the period before approximately 1870, before Abelam influences decisively affected Ilahita's social structure and demography. Thus, the Pre-Tambaran represents something of an ethnographic baseline from which to measure subsequent changes. The character of Ilahita society and culture during that period cannot be known directly, but is reconstructed from oral traditions and comparison with genetically related societies that received little or no Abelam influence.

- The *Tambaran* phase refers to the period between approximately 1870 and 1950. The significance of the latter date is that it marked the final cessation of traditional warfare. This was the phase of Ilahita's heyday of military, diplomatic, and ceremonial splendor. During this phase, also, increasing awareness of Europeans and other New Guinean peoples significantly intensified Ilahita's sense of its own cultural distinctiveness and identity, and the Tambaran emerged as an icon of Tradition – the personified mystique of a total way of life.

- The *Late Tambaran* phase refers to the period between 1950 and 1975, the year Papua New Guinea achieved national independence after more than a half-century of Australian rule. During this phase ceremonial life continued its traditional cycles, but with growing signs of fatigue and anachronism. The cessation of warfare removed the factor of greatest urgency in maintaining village size and solidarity, and small groups were no longer afraid to set up residential camps in Ilahita's hinterland. During this phase, also, a Christian mission arrived, as did cash cropping and the beginnings of Australian-sponsored democratic political institutions. Those novelties diverted time and attention away from the Tambaran. In response the cult elders, sensing the threat to their authority, increased the scope and stridency of Tambaran practices.

• The *Post-Tambaran* phase refers to the period from 1975 to 1984. The latter date is significant as the year when Tambaran secrecy was voluntarily destroyed by the men, putting an end to the cult and all of its associated practices. During this phase the Tambaran declined considerably as a result of the dying-off of traditional elders and the advent of a government school, a village court, expanded job opportunities outside the village, and the general empowerment of women. In fact, as a significant actor in village affairs the Tambaran was breathing his last when the men finally put him out of his misery.

The study foreshadowed

The following chapters tell Ilahita's story with respect to the ways in which external and internal events were interwoven to produce the evolutionary thrust of village society. Thus:

• Chapter 2 ("The setting") is a brief overview of the geographical location and subsistence regime of Ilahita, along with observations on the pronounced segregation of the sexes in this society. In addition to providing necessary background information, the point of the chapter is to show that there is nothing special in Ilahita's subsistence base or technology that would account for its unusual size and social complexity, as compared with other villages in the region.

• Chapter 3 ("History") focuses on Ilahita's variously traumatic and stimulating encounters with agencies of the world beyond its horizons: first contact with Europeans, World War II in the Sepik, the coming of a Christian mission, and the growing involvement with Western economic and political institutions. The information in this chapter forestalls any notion that Ilahita's social evolution, including certain ideological innovations concerning the Tambaran, was "pristine." The effects of outside influences have always been a part of Ilahita's evolutionary story, as told here.

• Chapter 4 ("How Ilahita got big") deals with the circumstances under which, in the nineteenth century, Ilahita underwent rapid population growth, the importation of Abelam institutions into Ilahita society, and the moral dilemma created by imposing a violent, misogynistic men's cult on an ancestral tradition that prescribed nurture and protectiveness on the part of men toward women. As in the colonial era that was to follow, external influences were decisive in Ilahita's evolutionary development. Also in this chapter, we learn that Ilahita's favorable geographical situation enabled it to take advantage of those external influences in ways that were not available to other villages in the region.

- Chapter 5 ("Residence structures") describes Ilahita's arrangement "on the ground" with particular reference to the problem of maintaining residential togetherness in the face of chronic tendencies toward division and fragmentation. The discussion deals with the special integrative challenges inherent in systems of "mechanical social solidarity."
- Chapter 6 ("The dual organization") presents the major structures of the Tambaran's dual organization, the details of which have evolved in direct response to the military need to maintain the social and residential integrity of this large village. The complexity of the system is shown in the way elaborate crosscutting structures bind together independent kinship, descent, and residence groupings, thereby overcoming the divisive tendencies identified in the preceding chapter.
- Chapter 7 ("The ritual road to hierarchy") sets Tambaran ideology and the dual organization "in motion" with illustrations of how these ideas and practices actually work to maintain the social and physical integrity of the village and to reproduce themselves. Attention to the internal dynamics of the dual organization shows how, through unconscious self-correcting mechanisms, the numerical balances on which the system depends are maintained against demographic effects that would tend to destabilize it. In the workings of the Tambaran, too, may be seen the emergence of hierarchical principles breaking free from this otherwise egalitarian "segmentary" society.
- Chapter 8 ("Conclusion") reviews Ilahita's evolutionary movements, but at a level of generality which notices that some of the major transitions undergone by that village have occurred in many times and many places in world history. In addition, the evolutionary potentials of mechanical social solidarity and egalitarian ideology are considered in the light of the Ilahita case.

2 The setting

Geography

On the map of the southwest Pacific region, the colossal island of New Guinea perches like a turkey hen just above the tip of the York Peninsula of northeastern Australia, peering west toward Indonesia (Map 1). In fact, the western half of the island – the head and breast of the turkey – is part of Indonesia. Formerly ruled by the Netherlands, as the remnant of its Dutch East Indies empire, western New Guinea was made a province of Indonesia and renamed Irian Jaya during the 1960s.

The eastern half of the island has a somewhat more complicated colonial history. During the 1880s, the northern part became a colony of Germany; in response, Great Britain appropriated the southern part (called "Papua" or "British New Guinea") and placed it under Australian administrative control. Following World War I, the Treaty of Versailles stripped Germany of its colonies, including its New Guinea colony, which the League of Nations (and later its successor, the United Nations) assigned to Australia as a "mandated trust territory." In 1975, the two areas of the Australian mandate joined together to become the independent nation of "Papua New Guinea." Unless otherwise indicated, this study deals with that nation, the eastern half of the *island* of New Guinea, without reference to Irian Jaya; and since our concern is with this area as a cultural and geographical region, rather than as a nation-state, "New Guinea" will be used, generically, to denote the entire eastern half of the island, including "Papua."

The world's second largest island (after Greenland), New Guinea is a "continental" island – so called because it is massive enough to generate its own weather patterns; it is 2,400 kilometers long and 800 kilometers wide – twice the land area of California, and half again the size of France. It is an island of great natural diversity, ranging from alpine meadows to majestic rainforests, steaming jungles and swamps, and stunningly beautiful

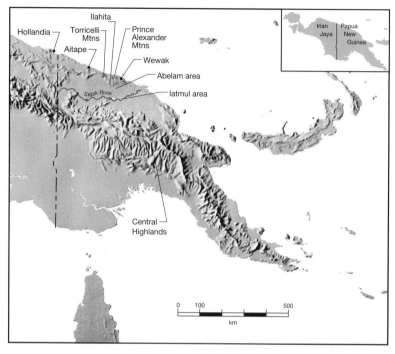

Map 1 Papua New Guinea

beaches. This diversity is matched by the many hundreds of distinct cultures inhabiting the island, separated into myriad large and small isolates by hostile neighbors and difficult terrain. Around the time the Australians took over, there were only about a million people living in the trust territory, and yet they spoke a thousand different languages, a sixth of the world's total.

The "backbone" of the island, known as the Highlands, is a vast array of high mountains and high valleys, stepping down into transitional, fringe zones on both north and south sides. With the introduction of the South American sweet potato, about 300 years ago (Hope and Golson 1995: 819), and the resulting explosion in the numbers of domesticated pigs, the central and western portions of the Highlands came to support some of the island's densest human populations. There, the settlement pattern consists mostly of dispersed homesteads or small clusters of related households known in the literature as "hamlets." Political leadership is based on the "big man" complex – a system in which men acquire prestige and followers not through inherited rank or wealth, but through skill as orators and entrepreneurs in the elaborate, large-scale pig exchanges. In the eastern

Highlands, population densities are almost as high, but settlements tend to be larger hamlets trending up to nucleated villages of a couple of hundred souls. Warfare is more dangerous and unrestrained than in the western Highlands (Feil 1987: 67) and exchange systems are less developed. Secret men's cults are prevalent, and ritual seniority is added to warriorship and other personal qualities as a basis for political leadership. The conditions and styles of leadership are sufficiently different, west to east, that the latter has come to be termed "great-man complex" to distinguish it from the "big-man complex" of the western Highlands (Godelier 1986; Godelier and Strathern 1991).[1]

On their southern side, the Highlands fall rather steeply to a broad lowland region, dominated by the great swamps and deltas formed by the Fly, the Purari, and other rivers as they meander their way to the Torres Strait, a water channel narrowly separating New Guinea from Australia.[2] Subsistence focuses on sago (see below), fishing, hunting, and, where conditions permit, gardening. Along the coast and in its nearby hinterland, populations are sizeable, large villages are not uncommon, and hereditary chiefdoms exist, as nowhere else in mainland New Guinea.

Beyond the northern fall of the Highlands lies another lowland region. There, streams also descend swiftly, but plunge as tributaries into the Ramu and Sepik rivers. One of New Guinea's four great rivers, the mighty Sepik rises in the far western Highlands, near the Irian Jaya frontier, descends steeply from its headwaters, and pursues a loopy, oxbow-littered course east–northeasterly to the northern coastline. From the mouth of the Sepik, all the way west along the north shore of the island, a series of coastal mountain ranges (the Prince Alexanders and Torricellis) – highlands not on the scale of the great central cordillera, but rugged enough in their own way – forms the northern rim of the Sepik basin. On their inland side, the mountains step down into a picturesque foothill region, which jumbles down into a grassy alluvial plain descending gradually to the Sepik river.

Significant in terms of agricultural adaptation is the fact that this plains area is subject to a pronounced wet and dry seasonality brought about by the weather shadow cast over the Sepik six months of the year by the great Highlands to the south. Thus, rain-laden southeast trade winds, blowing from October to March, drop their moisture in the high mountains before reaching the Sepik plains, leaving it to the northwest monsoon winds (April to September), which are not blocked by the lower-altitude coastal mountains, to deliver most of the region's approximately 175 centimeters of annual precipitation. Garden cycles depend on this seasonality, as do the kinds of crops that are able to grow here. Major work activities also step to this rhythm: the dry-season heavy labor of harvesting, clearing, and planting gardens is the responsibility of the men; once the rains begin, weeding and maintaining the gardens are women's work, while men spend much of their time in preparing ritual paintings, sculptures, and other paraphernalia for cult feasts and ceremonials in the following dry season, after the harvest.

Where the foothills meet the plains the terrain is broken by streams cutting their way southward from the coastal mountains; it is a patchwork zone of old rainforest, secondary forest, grass fields, and gardens. In some areas population densities rival those of the Highlands. The settlement pattern consists of relatively large, nucleated villages, the constituent hamlets of which are strung out along the ridge tops like beads on a necklace. Men's cults reign supreme in village ritual and social organization, and their towering spirit houses are masterpieces of artistic design and collective enterprise. Leadership is founded on the "great man" system of ritual excellence and seniority. This is the homeland of several cultural groups, including the Ilahita Arapesh, who are the subject of this study.

Numbering approximately 5,000 persons at the time of my original field work (1969–72), the Ilahita Arapesh are culturally and linguistically distinctive.[3] In all, they occupy seven villages divided into two opposed military alliances. Except during times of ritually sponsored truce, warfare in the form of raids, ambushes, and set battles was incessant – or, more precisely, the threat of attack was incessant. That is, until the Australians finally ended traditional warfare in the early 1950s. One of the alliances was dominated by the largest of the villages, Ilahita, from which the cultural group, including Ilahita village's enemies, takes its name. Indeed, with a population of 1,490 (in 1970), Ilahita is one of the largest traditional villages in all of New Guinea, which, as I mentioned previously, is what attracted me to study it in the first place.

This book, then, is about Ilahita and its surroundings: specifically, how this village got big, how it stayed big, how it came apart. These questions are not actually separable but are aspects of an evolutionary story that began over a hundred years ago, on the eve of Ilahita's stupendous growth and transformation. Before telling that story, let me offer some background facts, beginning with how, traditionally, the people made a living.

Gardening

Shortly before leaving Ilahita for the first time (1972), I was chatting with a group of men about my hopes for finishing my degree and obtaining a university teaching position, preferably in my homeland. My friends were interested (though not surprised) that students in America would be interested in learning about Ilahita. I took the opportunity to ask, "If I could tell the Americans only one thing about Ilahita, what should that be?" As one, the assembled men instantly replied: "Tell them we are mighty yam growers!"

Later, we will see why Ilahita men boast of themselves in such terms. For now, it is enough to say that the Ilahita are predominantly a horticultural people; their prowess at growing things is perhaps the source of their greatest pride and joy. One widely traveled geographer who visited the village remarked that their lush, manicured gardens were the finest he had seen in Papua New Guinea (William C. Clarke, pers. comm.). Like most tropical rainforest peoples who grow their own food, the Ilahita practice "slash-and-burn" (or "swidden") horticulture. This "extensive" form of cultivation involves clearing a garden-sized area of forest, allowing the cuttings to dry, and then burning them, thereby returning nutrients trapped in the foliage to the thin soil in the form of ash.[4] Some scorched, defoliated trees are left standing to serve as trellises for yam vines. The burst of fertility from the new ash supports yam cultivation in the first year, followed by other crops (e.g. banana, sugar cane, papaya) in the second and third years. By the third year, garden fertility is nearly depleted and natural reforestation is already under way. The ensuing fallow period lasts some twelve to fifteen years, before the cycle is repeated. This is a rolling cycle, in that a family clears new gardens every year and thus has gardens at each stage of development each year.

Two implications arise from the practice of slash-and-burn horticulture. The first is that a family's land resources must be extensive, many times greater than the amount utilized at any one time. The population density of groups practicing this technology is typically low to moderate, depending on a combination of factors: soil types, natural plant communities, technology, and social organization. If the ratio of human population to arable land rises for any reason,[5] strains usually develop: shorter fallow periods reduce garden productivity; newly perceived land shortages breed conflict within and between groups suddenly worried about ownership, trespass, and encroachment. The second implication of such systems is that settlements tend to be small and dispersed. As local settlement size increases, gardens must be cleared farther afield. Commuting distances increase, which is both a nuisance and, under conditions of chronic warfare and raiding, physically risky. For convenience, some families might stay in temporary garden huts during peak periods of activity. Eventually, some families decide that it would be handier to band together and establish a new settlement closer to their gardens; all the more so if there are tensions (as there usually are) in the mother village.

By means of such local movements, populations come to be dispersed on the land. In a later chapter, we will see that Ilahita village until recently impressively resisted this tendency toward fragmentation and dispersal.

How was this possible? We will see three factors at work: first, an accident of history and geography enabled its leaders to perceive the survival advantages of a large, defensible village; second, integrative structures emerging in step with increasing village population served to neutralize pressures that might otherwise have driven people apart; and, finally, the ideology of the men's cult exalted Ilahita village as a spiritual entity, conferring pride and security on those lucky enough to live there, and its rich ceremonialism made people want to be where the action was.

Foods

Garden foods chiefly consist of yam, taro, sugar cane, papaya, melons, squash, cucumber, a variety of leafy greens, and a tall grass known in Melanesian Pidgin as *pitpit* (*Saccharaum edule*), whose meaty inflorescence is highly tasty when roasted or mixed into soup.[6] Tree products include coconuts, breadfruit, banana, plantain,[7] the leaves and nuts from the small, spindly tulip tree (*Gnetum gnemon*) and various fruits and nuts of lesser dietary importance. Also grown, but not eaten in the usual sense, are: betel (or areca) nut, which grows on a slender palm, and which, when chewed with lime and the leaf of *Piper methysticum*, is mildly intoxicating; tobacco, a New World crop[8] introduced into the New Guinea region centuries ago by the Portuguese; and ginger, which is ingested for magical and medicinal purposes, rather than as a food or flavoring. By the mid-1980s coffee and cacao had become well-established as cash crops; cardamom, a spice, had been recently introduced and had yet to prove itself as a reliable source of income.[9]

For adults, animal protein – meat – is a relatively rare treat that is eaten mainly on ceremonial occasions. Some families raise one or two pigs, which they give, sell, or exchange to others; it is believed that eating one's own pig is like eating one's own child. This kindred sentiment also applies to wild pigs,[10] which provide most of the pork consumed. It is thought that the cult spirits, who supposedly materialize and eat the pork in the men's secluded presence, prefer the lean flesh of wild pigs to that of their village cousins. Hunting reserves are owned by particular ritual groups (see Chapter 6), which employ sturdy nets treated with proprietary magic to attract the "children" (pigs) to the nets of their "fathers" and to no others. Captured pigs are exchanged between ritual groups as part of the wider exchange of goods and services marking ceremonial occasions.

Other ground-dwelling animals – cassowary,[11] bandicoot,[12] and wallaby[13] – are caught with smaller, individually owned nets, and their consumption is not subject to ritual restrictions. Arboreal prey – tree kangaroos, smaller marsupials, some birds – are knocked off the limb with sticks or stones, while the hunter's human or canine helper waits below to finish them off when they fall. Smaller birds are caught by smearing sticky substances on the twigs where they are known to alight.

Some potential foods are not eaten because they are regarded as disgusting or because to do so would be undignified. Fishes, snakes, bats, and flying foxes (giant fruit bats) fall into this category, although large eels and pythons are eaten under ritual circumstances by very senior men, who, it is said, possess the "strength" necessary to withstand the powerfully dangerous spirits (*maolas*) that supposedly inhabit these animals. Other foods are eaten only by children. Lizards, locusts, and fledglings are the prey of these little hunters, whose tireless amusement at catching them[14] affords a steady high-quality protein intake superior to that of most adults – a crucial contributor to bodily growth, considering that children are unable to consume the substantial quantity of tubers and leafy greens needed to provide adequate vegetarian nutrition.

Another food to be mentioned is the sago grub, which, when roasted, is considered a delicacy, although some people report having an allergic reaction to eating it. These thumb-sized larvae of the rhinoceros beetle are obtained in large quantities from sago pulp which has been processed, heaped, and allowed to rot, as a medium for the larvae. This brings us to the subject of sago, which, along with yam, is Ilahita's staple food. We will need to know a good deal more about both sago and yams, since people in Ilahita think and talk about them constantly, and use them as metaphors for much else in their world.

Mother sago

The Ilahita tell a story about how sago came to be as it is. There was once a man and his wife who wanted to grow seedlings of a sago and a coconut. After planting, the woman guarded the sago seedling, the man the coconut seedling. At night, the woman fell asleep, allowing rhinoceros beetles to come and chew on the sprout. Ever since then, sago palms have grown into a squat, bushy shape. Being more disciplined, the man did not fall asleep, but remained vigilant, which is why coconut palms now grow straight and tall.[15]

Large tracts of lowland New Guinea are home to vast stands of sago palm (*Metroxylan sagu*). Preferring swampy conditions, sago is abundant in areas adjacent to waterways, where it can be amazingly prolific in establishing dense, impenetrable groves. Sago propagates both by sending out underground suckers and by producing a gigantic, once-in-a-lifetime flower, which eventually produces an estimated 900,000 seeds! For the Ilahita, the bushy shape of the sago palms, especially compared with coconut palms, together with their stupendous fecundity, are reason enough to regard them as both feminine and maternal; so is the fact that sago dwells in the dank, dark ("feminine") valley floors, whereas coconuts flourish where human settlements do – on the dry, sunlit ("masculine") ridge tops. The image of a plant encircled by its offspring – occurring also with taro, a root vegetable – is likewise suggestive to the Ilahita of something maternal; so, too, is sago's status as a wild thing that gives to human beings, while taking little in return, and never submits to full domestication (Tuzin 1992). Before addressing its symbolic aspects further, let me briefly describe how people get food from sago palms.

Sago palms are processed by family groups. Men and youths strip the large fronds from the plant, fell the trunk, peel back the skin, and pulverize the reddish-cream-colored pulp with adze-hafted stone hammers. Meanwhile, at the edge of the stream that is always nearby, women fashion troughs out of the large sago fronds. Elevated at the wider end, the trough is partitioned at waist-height by a sieve made from the burlap-like bast tissue of the palm. A catchment tub made from the palm's leathery spathe – the sheath that encloses the flower – is placed below the base of the trough. The woman repeatedly takes double handfuls of pulverized pulp, places them in the upper part of the trough, then washes them with water scooped from the stream, squeezing and kneading the soggy mass against the bast sieve. The rinse water passes down the trough and into the

Plate 6 Using adze-hafted hammers, men pulverize the soft interior of the sago palm.

Plate 7 During sago processing, the women's role is to wash the pulp using the trough-and-tub arrangement shown here.

Plate 8 At intervals, the woman pours the rinse water out of the catchment tub, exposing the white sago starch that has settled on the bottom.

catchment tub, carrying sago starch in suspension. At intervals the water is poured off, and the white starch-sediment is collected and carefully wrapped in banana leaves as family-meal-size "bricks," each weighing about two or three kilograms.[16] Most of the flour is consumed over a three-week period by the family that processed it, while some 20 percent is distributed in small packets to friends and family.

A man inherits sago palms from his father. Either they would be naturally occurring in a grove inherited by the father, or they would have been planted as seedlings by the father. A man may not eat sago he himself has planted, just as he may not eat his own pigs. Instead, the large job of clearing a grove site and defending the seedlings from jungle encroachment until they are big enough to fend for themselves must only be done as a gift to one's children and to more distant posterity. We will see that identifying certain foods as resources in which self-sufficiency is prohibited is a fundamental logic for integrating Ilahita social relations, and we will encounter this logic again and again.

Under normal conditions, a sago flowers after about sixteen years, and immediately dies. As if planning all its life for the Big Bloom, the palm steadily accumulates starch in its trunk. The trick, then, is to harvest the palm just before it blossoms, when the starch content is at its maximum, and before it is suddenly, dramatically expended in a glorious floral convergence of birth and death.[17] This moment, however, may not come at a time that is convenient for the owner: adequacy of current food supplies, along with the lack of techniques for storing sago flour for more than a couple of weeks, means that the owner will often prefer to give an about-to-flower palm to a friend, neighbor, or kinsman for whom the timing is more felicitous. Eventually, the gift will be reciprocated.

The resulting pattern of reciprocity forms the community into a dense thicket of exchange obligations in which precise accounting matters less than the idea that sago gifts are to be given and received fairly freely. Social relationships are thereby extended and reinforced, while the demand and supply of sago are maintained in an adaptive, efficient balance. In a later chapter we will see that the exchanging of like for like – sago for sago, yam for yam, sister for sister, et cetera – is the quintessential mechanism of what sociologists call *mechanical* (as opposed to *organic*) social solidarity (Chapter 5).

The physical and symbolic properties of sago, along with its role as an object of exchange, lend themselves to use by the men's cult, the Tambaran. That is to say, sago maternalism is revealed in the images attached to Falanga and Lefin, which are the two most junior (out of five) initiation grades of the Tambaran. Boys are initiated into these grades at about the ages of 5 and 9, respectively. The expressed purpose of the initiations is to open the path leading to manhood by violently separating the boys from women, especially from their mothers, whose breast milk is believed to have constituted their flesh. The ordeals consist of rubbing the boy's penis and scrotum with stinging nettles (Falanga) and slashing the boy's glans penis with a bamboo razor (Lefin). Both procedures are secrets not to be revealed to women, under pain of death. Instead, women are told that the boys are forced to shinny up a thorn-studded sago palm (of the variety known as *falanga*) and slide down, tearing their bellies in the process; as part of this symbolic linkage, it happens that *lefin* is the name given to sago as food. One could scarcely imagine more painful expressions (in both actual and figurative forms) of a boy's separation from his mother; it is the maternalism of sago that makes the symbolic connection.

In a far more benign mode, sago maternalism is displayed in a sentimental act performed by a man when he reaches an age that anticipates death. At that time he summons the sons of his sisters and offers them a mature sago palm, which they process and eat in a feast of fond farewell. The gift is a prepayment to these men for the last act of piety they will perform for their uncle, which is to bury him. In presenting his sisters' sons with the special sago, the celebrant reminds them that he "gave them their mothers." And in giving them their mothers, he also gave them their flesh, which is presumed to be inherited from the mother. Bone, which far outlasts flesh, is inherited from the father. It carries the spiritual essence of the line of descent traced through men – the patriline – a transmission made continuous during life by the eating of yams. Accordingly, we now consider yams in more detail.

Father yam

If the Arapesh are more than a little interested in sago, they are positively passionate about yams. The yams of which I speak are not the kind that fit easily on American platters at Thanksgiving, but are tubers of the genus *Dioscorea*. In Ilahita, small yams (primarily *D. esculenta*), reaching about 1–2 kilograms in weight, are the main daily fare, except during the two-to three-month interval when yams from the last harvest have run out and sago becomes the staple. Most varieties have flaky, white flesh that is slightly sweeter than an Irish or Idaho potato; others are more purplish, fibrous, or slightly bitter. Eaten roasted, boiled, or in thick soup laced with shredded coconut, these yams are delicious, to my taste, and I never tired of eating them.

Turning to the symbolic significance of yams, the first point to make is that yams are believed to have spirits. Small yams have spirits akin to those of (human) children, and indeed their behavior is said to be like that of an

Plate 9 Harvesting short yams. Here, a woman clips small rootlets off the tubers, prior to their being washed in a nearby stream.

Plate 10 Short yams are one of the main feast foods. Participants bring tubers, which are displayed in heaps before being redistributed for immediate consumption.

unruly gang of kids: capricious, playful, slightly naughty. If they find out they are about to be harvested, these yams are quite capable of fleeing the garden, leaving the harvesting party to poke about in the empty soil. Accordingly, a gardener intending to harvest on the next day keeps that fact to himself and quietly, even surreptitiously, places a magical "fence" around the garden, insuring that the pesky tubers will be there when he goes to collect them.

Long yams (*D. alata*) are another story entirely. These giants, reaching over 3 meters in length and over 70 kilograms in weight, possess spirits of great dignity and potential danger; appearing in dreams in their own or slightly disguised form, they literally summon the gardener to harvest. The dangerous aspect of these spirits (*maolas*) derives from the ashes of pythons or eels, long animals burnt as an ingredient of the magic used to grow long yams.[18] The benign aspect of long-yam spirits, on the other hand, arises from their companionship, on an invisible plane, with two other potent spirit types: those of the ancestral dead, and those of the men's cult, the Tambaran.[19]

Whence the startling idea that yams have spirits? The answer begins with the curious fact that yams, unlike other vegetables, are *artifacts*; that is, more than any other plant, they are fashioned. Local soils are dense and clayey; they must be softened if growing tubers are to penetrate them. In

Plate 11 Luxuriant yam vines point to an abundant harvest a few months later.

Plate 12 Long yams, appropriately decorated, are carried from the gardens for later, more elaborate, display.

Plate 13 Long yams being assembled for a secret Tambaran feast. During these conclaves, the non-initiates are told that the cult spirits assume material form and consume the feast.

planting a long yam, the gardener selects a secluded, sloping site, which he fences with a blind. At the entrance he places a leafy taboo marker, warning others, especially women, not to trespass. Using a secret technique known only to senior cult members, the man digs a shaft the size and shape of the desired yam. The backfill is carefully crumbled and replaced in the hole. The seed yam is placed atop the refilled hole and mounded over. A luxuriant vine grows up from the mound and sends nutrients down to develop the new tuber, which, following the path of least resistance, comes to fill the previous hole. In effect, then, the gardener digs a "mold" in the ground and "pours" the new yam into it, controlling the yam's ultimate size and shape. If a two-legged yam, or a yam with arms, is desired, this is achieved with appropriate side shafts in the initial excavation. By this means, the yam is more than a cultivated object; it is a work of personal expression, a work of art. Anatomically correct yams can and do occur and are objects of great interest and admiration. Given the amount of time invested in planting, tending, and harvesting these monsters, a man produces only one in a season.

Just as artists in Ilahita (and in our own society, at least in a metaphorical sense) consider that their creations are infused with their own (the artist's) spirit, so the spirits of these yams are embodiments of the gardener's own spirit; their majesty betokens the spiritual strength of

Plate 14 A display of their decorated long yams is mounted by the men of Ilifalemb ward. Admiring visitors are welcome!

the gardener. Long yams are dressed for display in headdress, feathers, paint, and shells, and they depict the ideal male: beautiful, strong, and virile – the male as the gardener thinks he is, or wishes to be.

This bodily identification of a man with his yams also betokens a spiritual continuity going back to the beginning of time. Because yams propagate vegetatively – that is, one gets a yam by planting a yam or part of a yam, not a seed – the yams you eat are the direct lineal descendants of the yams your ancestors ate. And because the Ilahita hold the idea that, as the Germans say, "you are what you eat" (*Man ist was Man isst*), eating one's ancestral yams is a sacramental ingesting of the same spiritual essences that one's ancestors ate and projected into the yams they grew. The lines of man and yam thus parallel and sustain each other through generations of spiritual ingestion, projection, and descent. In eating his yams, then, a man partakes of the spiritual essences of his ancestors, thereby becoming one with them.

Elsewhere (Tuzin 1972), I have analyzed yams as phallic symbols. Here, it is enough to say that the strong emotional identification of men with their yams energizes an elaborate system of yam displays, competitions, and alliances, which, as described in a later chapter, is a key contributor to village security and solidarity. Such an institution would not be possible without two factors of paramount importance about yams: they can be produced in *surplus* quantities far exceeding subsistence demand, and they are *storable*.[20] Only with surpluses can the village support the stupendous displays, feasts, and giveaways which, as we will see, are the centerpiece of social life in its public aspects. Yam cultivation – with or without surpluses – depends, in turn, on favorable environmental conditions, in particular, the pronounced wet–dry seasonality that prevails in this part of the Sepik region. Only with storability can a man's or a community's entire year's crop of yams be displayed all at once. Whereas Highlands sweet potatoes (*Ipomoea batatas*) perish quickly, such that planting, harvesting, and eating them are continuous activities, and "storing" them is achieved only by converting them into pigs – the Highlanders' passion – in Ilahita (and some other yam-growing areas in New Guinea and West Africa) yams are the unmediated symbol of masculine prestige, power, and potency.

The striking gender symbolism of yams and sago draws attention to a pattern that is deeply embedded in the culture of Ilahita and of many other tropical horticultural peoples: the sexual division of labor. Although certain tasks (e.g. roasting tubers) are indifferent to this division, others are so strictly aligned as to be part of the very definition of gender. In general, men's tasks are those that are heavy or dangerous (e.g. felling large trees, hunting, planting and harvesting yams, making war), while women's work tends to be tedious or repetitive (e.g. carrying water, firewood, and garden produce, sweeping and weeding the garden). Both men and women are strongly committed to this gendered arrangement, such that great shame and pity occurs when circumstances, such as the death of a spouse, force a person to perform tasks appropriate to the opposite sex. It is not only labor that is organized along the lines of sex and gender. Sexuality is the template for many gendered social and ideological distinctions, so much so that it could be said that the Ilahita, like many other New Guinea societies, inhabit a "gender-inflected universe" (Lindenbaum 1987: 222). The gravitational forces of this universe pull at the individual from an early age.

Gender inflections

A baby is a baby; it needs to be fed, held, cuddled, kissed, bounced, tickled, and talked to. As far as I could observe, Ilahita boys and girls are both treated this way during the first three years of life. Three years is the average nursing period, during which the mother must not have sexual intercourse, lest (it is believed) the semen infiltrate her breast milk and injure the nursling. The weaning of the child and the resumption of marital sex mean that a new pregnancy will soon follow, sustaining a clockwork birth interval of four years – a pattern evident in the genealogical record. For the weanling, the trauma of weaning is that of immediately losing both the breast and the undivided attention of its mother, who now sleeps with her

Plate 15 A baby needs to be cuddled.

husband rather than with the baby, followed about a year later by being displaced by a greedily suckling next-born.[21] In nutritional terms, the weanling enters a two- to three-year period of dietary hardship, since it no longer nurses nor is it big enough to eat the quantity of carbohydrate foods needed to thrive on this diet. Next to the early days just after birth, the period of weaning is normally the time of highest mortality.

During the toddler stage (approximately 3–6 years of age), boys and girls gradually diverge in their behaviors and in the way others behave toward them. Systematic observations of crying and fretful behavior, for example, suggest that little boys experience more craving and frustration than little girls do, when it comes to the need for attention from their mothers (Tuzin 1997: 226). Toddlers of both sexes continue to accompany their mothers to the gardens. But whereas little girls are taught scaled-down versions of the women's work of weeding, sweeping, and carrying, little boys occupy themselves at play, usually under the eye of a babysitting older sister or girl-cousin. Toward the end of the weanling period, a boy frequently will remain back in the village, hanging out with the older boys, while a girl his age continues at her mother's side, gradually acquiring the muscles, know-how, and forbearance of a woman.

The developmental separation of the sexes radically increases at about age 5, when the boys are initiated into Falanga and, some years later, Lefin, the two lowest grades of the Tambaran. In addition to the genital ordeals mentioned earlier, the boys are secluded with the men for several weeks, entrusted with minor secrets, and given items of cult paraphernalia (e.g. bullroarers[22]) associated with the grade. These initiation experiences dramatically affect boys' attitudes toward women, especially their mothers.

Probably in most societies, boys at this age struggle to separate themselves, physically and psychologically, from their mothers. In Ilahita, this process is massively buttressed by the full force and majesty of the Tambaran's female-hating ideology. Thenceforward, in countless ways, they are reminded that they are men-in-training. Women, it is said, are the bane of male society, the source of much discord, and they represent a threat to masculine vitality, solidarity, and enterprise. The same lesson is repeated at the third-grade initiation, Maolimu, during which adolescent youths are ritually secluded for several months in a secret "village" in the forest, erected for the purpose. The women are told that the young men are transformed into flying foxes – proverbially lusty creatures – and that the whoops and howls faintly echoing from the distant forest are the sounds of celebration over the many (human) women brought there to satisfy the initiates' stupendous sexual appetites.[23] In actuality, it is not women but pigs that are brought to them, as part of a ritual campaign to teach them to crave pork – a manly passion – by gorging and essentially transforming themselves with it. As in the case of yam sacramentalism, the men *are* what they eat; hence the kinship that binds men, yams, and pigs together.

With these ritual experiences of childhood and adolescence behind them, males are predisposed to understand and accept the masculinist doctrines of Nggwal, the two highest grades of the Tambaran. Specifically, entry into Nggwal Bunafunei corresponds with a man's entry into adulthood; Nggwal Walipeine, the tambaran of old men, is normally achieved at about the age of 45–50. Many men die before reaching Nggwal Walipeine; and very few men indeed live beyond the age when their cohort passes Nggwal Walipeine on to their junior initiation partners. Those frail few who do pass out of the "top" of the system are truly retired and powerless; indeed, they are socially dead.

*****

In many respects traditional Ilahita is typical of village communities located in tropical forest areas. Its general features are found throughout much of cultural Australasia, the Pacific islands, lowland Amazonia, and central and western Africa: subsistence horticulture based on tubers and palms; gardens grown with slash-and-burn techniques and rotations, supplemented with products of the forest; tools and weapons made of stone, wood, and vegetable fibers; a social organization based on kinship and descent, with corporate identity residing in totemic clans, subclans, or other such groups; a relatively egalitarian ethos, with an emphasis on gift exchange and the sharing of necessities; a political system favoring age and personal leadership qualities rather than inherited rank; a pronounced sexual division of labor, extending to gender inflections in many ideas and practices, including a ritual system based on a men's cult; and inter-community warfare and distrust as the normal state of affairs.

This list of typical features implies that, in seeking to account for Ilahita's singular size and organizational complexity, even as compared with other villages in the immediate vicinity, we cannot appeal to differences in technology, ecology, or basic social institutions. We will see in Chapter 4 that Ilahita did benefit, in fact, from a favorable geographical location, which very likely set this village on the road to the development of unusual social complexity. Once launched, however, the development itself was propelled largely by ideological and organizational dynamics. That is to say, *upon* the foundational elements listed above, Ilahita in its heyday evolved to a level of scale and complexity unprecedented, as far as I am aware, among societies of its type. It was not always this way. In the next chapter we begin to explore the events and processes that made it so.

3   History

Experiencing the alien

Certain popular films and books belong to a science-fiction genre which invites us to imagine what it would be like if we were to establish contact with intelligent, extraterrestrial life. Death rays and eerie music aside, if such an event were to occur it would boggle the mind of terrestrial philosophy and religion. The discovery that WE ARE NOT ALONE IN THE UNIVERSE! would be nothing less than a discovery of *ourselves* – a new level of self-awareness, self-identification, and self-objectification, the magnitude and significance of which would dwarf the cosmologies of Galileo and Copernicus, and would swallow whole the lump raised in the throat by the Apollo photograph of the Earth rising over the Moon.

Imagine, then, Ilahita – about a hundred years ago. According to the old people, in those days the Ilahita believed that the world ended at the horizon, and that folks who lived at the horizon spent their time cutting the sky away from the earth, to maintain the separation. The sky was not so high: the sun, moon and stars in the firmament rode just above the highest treetops; meteors were the spirits of the recent dead as they flitted from one abode to the next. Although a walk of two to three days north into the mountains would have brought an Ilahita traveler to within sight of the Bismarck Sea, they were not aware of its existence; seashells (conch, nautilus, trochus, cowrie, shell rings cut from giant clams) found their way into the interior and were valued by the Ilahita as much for their mysterious origins as for their beauty and purity. Rumor had it that a great waterway (the Sepik river) lay to the south; but no villager had seen it, or knew anyone who had. In the late nineteenth century Malay plume hunters from the west may have come to within about 30 kilometers of Ilahita; but, although certain Malay influences reached Ilahita – for example, the Ilahita word for "white man," *dowank*, is almost certainly a cognate of *tuan*, the Malay word for "lord" – there is no tradition that the hunters had been met or rumored about at the time. At the dawn of the twentieth century, then, the Ilahita cosmos was very small, both physically and cognitively.

The first inkling that they might not be "alone" came to Ilahita during the first decade of the twentieth century – during "German time," as the villagers now call that era. An armed European patrol skirted the western edge of Ilahita territory. Their mission is not known. An Ilahita family spotted the patrol from their garden; ready to protect his family, the man menaced them from across a small river with his spear, and was shot dead. The patrol continued south and killed a few persons from other villages, before exiting the area toward the east. It was presumed that these human-ish strangers, with their miraculous weapons and startling ability to take off and put on their "skins" casually and at will, were ghosts (also called *dowank*, which is synonymous with the traditional term, *gamba*) – not really outsiders at all, but "inside aliens," so to speak, visitors from within a normally invisible sector of Ilahita's own cramped cosmos. Still, the experience did crack that cosmos, just a little.

Plate 16 The Nanu river west of Ilahita, near the spot where an armed German patrol shot and killed an Ilahita man early in the twentieth century.

War and the end of war

The next time Ilahita directly experienced outside contact was in 1936, when the village was visited by an Australian police patrol. The Australians were there to track down and capture the killers of Charlie Gough, a labor recruiter. Charlie had been breaking the rules by patrolling in "uncontrolled territory." In exchange for a few trade goods, he recruited a number of young men from Lehinga village, Ilahita's neighbor and traditional enemy to the east. A day into their journey to the coast, one of the recruits became homesick and fled back home. Foolishly, Gough followed him there. As he went to apprehend the runaway, he was speared to death by the young man's kinsmen.

Word of the killing reached the Australian administration in Wewak (Map 1). A police patrol was mounted. They arrived in Lehinga to find the village nearly deserted, and to learn that the men they were after had fled west toward the big village of Ilahita. As the patrol approached Ilahita, they were met at the outskirts of the village by a delegation of leaders. The officers announced that they and their large company of (hungry, randy) carriers and constables would be staying in Ilahita for as long as it would take to catch the fugitives, and that they would require the village's hospitality. The bluff – if it *was* a bluff – worked: the Ilahita leaders replied that if the patrol would only camp *outside* the village, they (the Ilahitans) would find the Lehingans for them. And that is what they did, in very short order.[1]

The Maprik post (Map 2) was established in 1937 to extend the rule of law into this "wild" region of New Guinea; to oversee the recruitment of laborers for coconut plantations on the coast and offshore islands; and to provide administrative services to prospectors, who were arriving in response to gold's having been discovered in the Prince Alexander mountains.[2] A few years after the Gough incident, some young Ilahita men signed up for one- or two-year stints on the plantations. Before they could return with news and goods of the outside world, World War II arrived in New Guinea, delaying their homecoming for several years.

Early in 1942, shortly after their attack on Pearl Harbor, the Japanese invaded and occupied coastal and insular parts of northeastern New Guinea, from which they launched bombing raids on northern Australia. By 1944, Allied forces under General Douglas MacArthur had succeeded in cutting the Japanese maritime supply lines, isolating and starving them on the New Guinea islands and mainland in anticipation of ground assaults. On the Sepik coast, the Japanese commandant at Wewak (Map 2) reacted by sending troops over the mountains, into the interior, there to live off the gardens and await the final showdown. Accordingly, in July

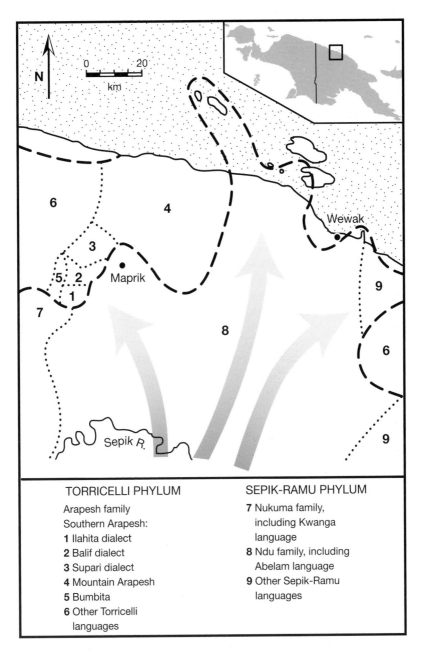

TORRICELLI PHYLUM

Arapesh family
Southern Arapesh:
1 Ilahita dialect
2 Balif dialect
3 Supari dialect
4 Mountain Arapesh
5 Bumbita
6 Other Torricelli
languages

SEPIK-RAMU PHYLUM

7 Nukuma family,
including Kwanga
language
8 Ndu family, including
Abelam language
9 Other Sepik-Ramu
languages

Map 2 Languages of the Maprik–Wewak area (after Laycock 1973)

1944, just as Ilahita was about to launch an attack against an enemy village, a large force of Japanese infantry appeared, announced that they had come to liberate the people from Euro-Australian tyranny, quashed Ilahita's battle plans, and made themselves at home.

For a while, everything went well. The Japanese soldiers were recruited from among the very young by that late stage of the war. The villagers felt sorry for them and virtually adopted them into their families. The soldiers, many of whom had been farm boys themselves, helped in the gardens, and even introduced some new crops, such as cassava. Then, after the Allied landing at Aitape (Map 1), the Australians crossed the coastal range and began sweeping easterly through the hinterland, looking for Japanese units and conducting aerial bombardments in advance of infantry attacks. As the fighting drew closer, some young village men were recruited by the advancing Australians to be spies and saboteurs; they were given hand grenades and were instructed in their use. Relations between the Japanese and the villagers turned very ugly (Tuzin 1983). Through their agents the Australians sent word ahead, advising people to flee their villages in advance of bombing sorties; many had already done so, and those that hadn't, did. Significantly, not knowing how long they might have to remain in hiding, the villagers planted coconuts in their forest refuges; grown to maturity, these coconuts were destined to become the start of permanent, outlying settlements long after the war had ended.

In late January 1945, Australian infantry took Ilahita after a battle lasting three days.[3] As the campaign swept eastward toward Wewak, people drifted back to start rebuilding their ruined village. Ironically, perhaps, it was the Japanese who initially put a stop to traditional warfare, and, after all the carnage they had just witnessed, the Ilahita had no stomach for resuming it. Quarrels, lawsuits, fights, even *ad hoc* raiding continued between enemy villages, virtually up to the present; but serious, organized warfare designed to annihilate enemy lives and property – that became a thing of the past. As we will see in a later chapter, the end of endemic warfare was to have decisive effects on the viability of Ilahita as a village.

The Mission

After the war, it took a few years for conditions to return to normal and for the Australian civilian administration to be restored. Then, in 1952, another exogenous event of potentially great magnitude occurred: Christian missionaries arrived in Ilahita. This was the South Sea Evangelical Mission (SSEM), a Protestant-Evangelical organization begun in the early years of the twentieth century to service Solomon Islanders working on the sugar plantations of Queensland (Australia). Eventually, when the workers returned home, the SSEM followed them back to the Solomons; then, after World War II, the mission spread to the Ilahita area. It so happens that, for at least the first two decades of their presence, the missionaries actually living in Ilahita were of German nationality, members of evangelical sects allied with the SSEM.

By 1969, when I first arrived in Ilahita, the Mission compound included a small church, a small clinic, a small boarding school that taught basic literacy skills, and four personnel: an about-to-retire female teacher who headed the station, two young female nurses, and one young male teacher. All four of these workers were active proselytizers of Christianity; but, interestingly, nearly all their efforts were directed at *other* villages in the vicinity, not at Ilahita itself. Although Ilahita was described in SSEM publications as "the Stronghold of Satan," resident missionaries treated the village more as their base of operations rather than as their principal target of evangelizing work. That is one of the reasons for the remarkably slight effect the SSEM had had on life in Ilahita. By 1969, after seventeen years of missionization, only 15 percent of adults professed to be Christians; another 9 percent were admitted backsliders, who had become disillusioned with Christianity when the material rewards they were expecting failed to materialize.

Another reason for the Mission's relative lack of success in converting villagers to Christianity was the robust effectiveness, during the first two decades of Mission presence, of the Tambaran, and the powerful interests that were vested in it. In addition to claims that the men's cult, through the magic of its rituals, was the source of all village prosperity, it was the chief institution of social control. The men, especially the older men, knew that the Tambaran was the only instrument they had for imposing their will on others and safeguarding their own welfare. Theirs was an urgent, intolerant insistence that Tambaran ceremonialism and associated practices be maintained against all forces that would threaten them, including Christianity.[4]

The final reason for the Mission's minimal impact was that it demanded too much of its converts. Unlike the Catholic Society of the Divine Word mission that was active in other parts of the Sepik, which saw many traditional practices as religiously neutral, innocuous, or even useful for their purposes, the austere Protestants of the SSEM saw virtually all of tradition as part of Satan's Project. In addition to prohibiting converts from participating in cult activities, the Mission tabooed smoking, betel-nut chewing, competitive gardening, life-change ceremonies, body ornaments, dancing, nudity – which was customary in former days – artistic activity, polygyny,[5] and oratory in the traditional style of formal harangue. Faced with giving up practically everything that lent meaning, color, pageantry, and enjoyment to life, in favor of a foreign doctrine promising rewards that appeared to Ilahitans, to say the least, distant and ethereal, the great majority of villagers chose to stay as they were.

If the advent of Christianity and its emissaries did not trigger immediate, mass conversions among the villagers, the event nonetheless had profound long-term effects on Ilahita society and culture. First, the SSEM's provision of clinical services, especially in the area of mother and infant care, its advice to reduce the lactation interval, and its silence on birth-control measures – all of these set the demographic stage for a population explosion starting in the mid-1970s. As envisaged in the previous chapter, upsetting the delicate balance between population and productive resources (land, food trees) deleteriously affected both the subsistence system and the social system, creating strains that seriously undermined village welfare and solidarity.

Secondly, the advent of this other belief system, one that offered an alternative explanation for life and death, blessings and sufferings, augmented the condition of self-objectification that had received a qualitative boost when the people of Ilahita first encountered white men.[6] They say that it will not be a fish that discovers water. Christianity enabled the Ilahita to "discover" the Tambaran, in the sense that it suddenly rendered this institution less transparent, less taken-for-granted, to its adherents. The immediate effect of this confrontation was to intensify and formalize the Tambaran, clarifying and in a sense *creating* a tradition identified as *non*-White, *non*-Christian.

From another point of view, this intensification reflected a new, more urgent sense of Tambaran orthodoxy, as cult leaders moved to protect their authority and the way of life of which they were custodians. The maneuver succeeded for about twenty years, long enough for the senior cult elders to reach their graves. Then, with the turning of the generations and the testing of this cultural self-object, based on the Tambaran, against rapidly modernizing conditions, the identity edifice collapsed. That is the way with strategies which define the self as an object – a thing with boundaries and an identity – whether the self-object in question is a culture or an individual: the qualities of clarity and commitment that make the "objects" effective in the short run, render them brittle, less absorptive, and less able over the long run to adapt to changing circumstances.

Finally, there is the matter of the devastating version of Christianity to which mission Christianity eventually led, albeit inadvertently. From the start of missionization in Ilahita the aspirations of Christian converts focused not so much on the spiritual rewards promised in the Gospels, as on the prospect of lavish material rewards. A widespread, much written-about belief among many New Guinea peoples is that the Bible holds the key to the fabulous wealth – the "cargo" – of the Europeans. This belief has inspired many variants of a practice known as "cargo cult," whereby ritual, magical, and behavioral procedures are deployed in the hope of bringing the "cargo" to the people (Lawrence 1964). Ilahita dabbled in such practices during the 1950s and 1960s, but to no avail. After a few failed attempts, most villagers became disillusioned and skeptical; but cargoistic thinking persisted, especially among the tiny band of Christian converts.

As the years wore on, these converts grew increasingly impatient that *mission* Christianity perennially failed to deliver the goods, and that village traditionalists were never punished for their heathenism. By the late 1970s, it was clear to them that the Christianity they had been taught was seriously flawed (or dishonest) and that a radically new approach was needed. Accordingly, a new, widely supported movement arose in the early 1980s known as the Revival. Anti-White and anti-Mission in sentiment, and with distinct cargoistic overtones, this movement sought to cleanse the village of all Satanic beliefs and practices, thus clearing the way for a Happening of cosmic proportions: the advent of heaven on earth, possibly in the person of Jesus Christ, but clearly involving the acquisition of great riches.[7]

For this scenario to occur, something had to be done about the Tambaran. Bristling with features now seen to be devil-worshipping, indeed Satanic, it was the personification of virtually all things traditional, was firmly associated with war and sorcery and human sacrifice, had resisted the penetration of Christianity into village life, and had stood in the way of modernity. The Tambaran had to go. And so, on an afternoon in September 1984, the Tambaran was killed, when, by prearrangement, a group of men revealed the cult secrets to an assemblage of women. On that day, Ilahita's "ethnographic present" became its past, and a new historical epoch began.[8]

Coffee, councils, and courts

The revelation of cult secrets and the destruction of the Tambaran would not have been politically possible, were it not for many exogenous, secular changes that had occurred in Ilahita during the preceding period. The introduction of cash was perhaps the most significant of these changes. Like colonial authorities elsewhere, the Australians, in order to develop New Guinea's economy, instituted a "head tax" in each new area that came under their control. Never mind that the tax was very small; what mattered was that it could only be paid in cash. Initially, the only way to obtain cash was to work for Europeans, which is how the nascent plantation economy obtained its laborers. By the 1950s, it was a matter of routine for young

Ilahita men to spend one or two stints on the plantations – drawn more by the bright lights of the outside world, than by the desire to raise cash to give to their relatives back home. With money left over after taxes, villagers could buy steel tools, clothing, rice, tinned fish, salt, soap, razors, and other goods, offered for the most part by Chinese traders who set up small shops at commercially strategic locations. A taste was created for goods that only cash could buy, and from then on it was only a matter of time before Cash would be King.

The next stage in the developing economy was to promote the growing of crops that could be sold for cash, as an independent source of income in the rural areas. During the 1960s, agricultural extension officers taught the Ilahita to grow peanuts and dry rice, neither of which proved ultimately successful as a cash crop. Coffee, on the other hand, flourished under local growing conditions and, despite sharp fluctuations in world coffee prices, yielded a good return on (mostly women's) labor and the necessary transportation investment. By the late 1970s, cacao (chocolate) had become second to coffee as Ilahita's main source of cash.

The problem with coffee and cacao was that their groves required sizeable land acreage – land previously used for food gardens, or land that had to be cut from forested hunting reserves. The Ilahita, who were accustomed to slash-and-burn technology, were disconcerted when the garden rotation returned to land that, in the meanwhile, had been planted with coffee or cacao trees, crops which produce not for a year or two, but for decades. Land for food gardens had to be created by clearing areas of old forest or by shortening the fallow period, neither of which was an attractive prospect. The process initiated was one that is dismally typical of the so-called Third World: rural villagers are induced to spend more of their time and resources on cash-cropping, less on subsistence farming, in order to spend much of their money on – what? Food! And, of course, consumer goods. In the absence of expanded opportunities for capital investment by individuals or collectives, the growth of a cash economy can be, as it has been in Ilahita, a mixed blessing.

A major sociological effect of cash-cropping has been the unseemly scrambling of individuals to obtain *personal* title to as much land as possible. In the old days, although land was owned by descent groups, "ownership" was far less important than the security of having the *use* of land sufficient to one's gardening needs, thus motivating people to maintain their kinship relationships in good order. Even allowing for the competitive desire to plant as many yams as possible, under conditions where land was abundant and was exclusively a subsistence resource, there was a practical limit to the amount of land any individual could use. When land became a source of *cash*, however, all that changed; for there is no limit to the

Plate 17 Nowadays, store-bought rice and tinned fish, not yams, are the main feast food. Another change is the occasional use of corrugated iron for house roofs and walls.

amount of cash one might desire and be able to use. As land took on this new value, aided by the national government's program of granting legal title to fixed pieces of real estate, principles of collective ownership rapidly gave way to individual ownership, as a kind of "privatization." In the process, collective identity was, itself, undermined, and the individual was no longer so beholden to the group.

Meanwhile, as the importance of cash increased in the village, jobs outside were no longer restricted to those of unskilled, low-paid plantation laborers. With the developing economy, employment as tradesmen, drivers, factory and construction workers, clerks, etc., was increasingly available to enterprising young men and women. The scope for employment increased to the managerial level as educational opportunities increased. In 1975, a government school covering the first six grades was opened in Ilahita. Each year, a few of the best students leave to attend boarding high schools in Maprik, Wewak, and elsewhere. From there, some will enter college, the military, or some other training facility; others will go straight into prestigious jobs; few will return to Ilahita to plant yams. It is a pattern that has been repeated many times in many places in the developing world.

During the 1970s, these economic activities increasingly drew time and attention away from the Tambaran. With the advent of the government school, basic education became virtually universal among village young-sters, who were no longer available to the Tambaran for long periods of ritual seclusion. With education and government-sponsored programs such as family planning and women's cooperatives, women became more assertive and less willing to be quite so intimidated by men in the name of the Tambaran. Under these varied conditions the Tambaran, under the stewardship of the old men, became feeble and toothless and unwanted in its own home – almost dead, in fact. That is why the Revivalists, when the moment came, were able to kill it.

Among the casualties of increasing cash and educational opportunities was the traditional system of sister-exchange marriage. Formerly, the only way for a man to obtain a wife was to give a sister in exchange.[9] To get married, then, a young man required the assistance and goodwill of others: his father, for making the arrangements for him, usually while he and his future wife were children; his future father-in-law, for cooperating in this arrangement; his future brother-in-law, for carrying out his part of the bargain, when the time of marriage was nigh; and, of course, his sister, for cooperating with the whole arrangement and not allowing her affections to stray. At the time of my first field work (1969–72), villagers knew that many other New Guinea groups practiced brideprice – the giving of wealth to a would-be wife's kinsmen – but they were morally repelled by the idea, which they believed treated women as chattels. "Women are too precious to buy," said one man. "To get a woman, you should have to give a woman." Upon returning to the field (1985–6), I found that sister-exchange marriage was fast becoming extinct. Young people were balking at the tra-dition of arranged marriage; and a man who had money could now be a free agent in the marriage market.[10] Marriage, in a word, like land ownership, was becoming "privatized."

Another dimension of change during this modernizing period was political. During the 1960s, as a prelude to national independence and as a way to instill democratic ideas in the populace, the Australian adminis-tration instituted local-government councils in the Sepik region. Villagers elected one of their own to be their local-government councilor; Ilahita's large size entitled it to two such functionaries. In the early days of this institution, councilors tended to be young men who spoke good Melanesian Pidgin, would be clever at representing the village to Australian authori-ties, and would not be a threat to the sovereignty of the cult elders over matters of more traditional concern. The office of village councilor had limited responsibilities: organizing community work projects one morning a week, adjudicating minor disputes, and acting as a communication conduit between the government and the village. But in time, as traditions waned and attention turned more toward the external world of business, government, and education, election to the office of village councilor could launch a career of influence and material prosperity.

Of somewhat greater consequence was the instituting of village courts at the time of national independence in 1975. The system effectively combines Euro-Australian legal principles, inside knowledge of relevant customs and personalities, and enforcement measures backed up by the state. Each jurisdiction (usually a cluster of several villages) elects a court of three magistrates, a clerk, and a bailiff, who are then formally trained for their positions. At its fortnightly sessions, the village court hears cases ranging from the trivial to the quite serious. Up to certain limits, the magistrates are authorized to levy fines, court costs, and jail terms. The court's power is real. Many of the cases are creatures of modern conditions: domestic strife, at a time when women are asserting themselves for the first time; youth delinquency, at a time when the elders are losing control of the society; violations of contractual agreements, at a time when cash is introducing novel business arrangements, often at the expense of customary social relationships.

In all, the greatest effect of the village court system has been to shift legal identity from the collective (a patriline, clan, or subclan) to the individual. It used to be that a person who was wronged could depend on

Plate 18 Magistrate Kunai (in white shorts) presides over the Ilahita village court, while the ethnographer (bearded, on right) records the proceedings.

Plate 19 With the ritually-based authority of the cult elders now a thing of the past, fistfights among the young men are frequent and relatively uncontrolled.

Plate 20 Kotawa frowns as she watches an ugly shouting match develop between young men at a meeting of Ililip ward's coffee cooperative.

others of his social group to defend or avenge him; indeed, it used to be that a man (or woman) would rarely act in his own interests, but would sit aside, knowing that his fathers or brothers or cousins would do so on his behalf. In such a society, it pays to keep one's kinship relationships in good working order, to come to a brother's defense knowing that you may be calling upon him, someday, for assistance. Today, the whole matter of legal responsibility devolves upon the individual. If you are wronged and go to your brother for help, his response will be, "Take him to court!" The institution that created this new consciousness stands ready to service it. This change is one of great sociological moment, for it describes a movement from family-based kinship to state-based citizenship as the prime element in the legal constitution of the person. As with others already mentioned, this movement has occurred in many places and periods in human history, and has played a large part in the making of the modern world.

How Ilahita got big

Prehistory in the strict sense

In Chapter 1, I referred to the difficulty ethnographers have in discovering the unwritten past of a non-literate society, and yet some picture of how things used to be is essential if we are to interpret how they came to be different at a later time. While archaeologists and palaeontologists use physical remains to track evolutionary change, ethnographers have only what people tell them. It is bad enough that events within living memory can be mis-remembered, lied about, or simply forgotten; when it comes to events beyond living memory, worse difficulties arise. Plausible "oral histories" must often be assessed in the light of current claims; informants may or may not be faithfully reporting what their fathers told them – whatever distortions *that* may have involved. So, if two groups are contesting ownership of a certain piece of land, the stories each tells of how its ancestors came to acquire the land must be assessed in the light of possible bias, deliberate or not.

By testing competing accounts for internal consistency and coherence with related cultural ideas, the investigator can usually produce a best guess of what actually happened. And yet, by definition, such memories and such histories are recognizable in terms of *today's* society. Actors and ethnographers can relate to them, because the events occurred within a cultural setting not too dissimilar from today's. Those aspects that *are* highly dissimilar are those the storyteller first ignores and first forgets. Alternatively, the "remembered" setting may be so radically different as to be fantastical, in which case the memory has passed over into the realm of myth. Mythic accounts can rarely be accepted at face value; the story about how sago and coconut palms came to be tells us more about Ilahita gender notions than it does about palaeobotany – a service not without its merits, but not having much to do with history, either.

To obtain a credible picture of a society in a *previous form* – which is our ambition in this chapter – one turns to cultural comparison. In comparing cultures for the purposes of historical insight, linguistic affinities are especially helpful, since they are among the best evidence of a common ancestral culture.[1] In Chapter 2, it was noted that the Ilahita dialect belongs to one of three languages that comprise the Arapesh family, the distribution of which is shown on Map 2. By comparing standard wordlists and applying various analytic techniques, linguists Glasgow and Loving (1964: 8) have shown that the Ilahita language is much more closely related to Mountain Arapesh than to Bumbita Arapesh, even though Ilahita territory is adjacent to that of the Bumbita and widely separated from that of the Mountain Arapesh. This Arapesh family of three languages in turn belongs to the large Torricelli language phylum, members of which are distributed throughout the coastal Torricelli mountains and interior foothills, generally west and northwest of Ilahita. Ndu family languages (Map 2), on the other hand, are completely unrelated to any of the Torricelli languages, but do show close affinities with languages along the Sepik river proper.

The geographical distribution of all these languages suggests that not too long ago – a few centuries, judging from rate-of-change assumptions applied to the wordlist data – Arapesh speakers occupied a long, unbroken segment of the Prince Alexander and Torricelli foothills–plains transition zone. The mountains themselves are sufficiently rugged and unfit for human habitation that it is unlikely they would have been used for anything other than hunting and foraging expeditions; communication with the coast was likely to have been infrequent or non-existent.[2] Then, at some historical period, all of this changed. Ndu speakers entered the region from the south, drove a wedge between Arapesh speakers, and extended on over the mountains to the coast. Some Arapesh speakers apparently moved to the mountains and/or the coast, not by choice, but because they were displaced from their homelands deeper in the interior.[3] As certain as it is that these movements took place, they are not remembered by the Ilahita, who learned only about fifty years ago that speakers of a language (Mountain Arapesh) quite similar to theirs, live far to the east, on the other side of their Ndu-speaking neighbors, the Abelam.

How did these movements occur? Chances are, they happened gradually, over a period of generations. The northward movement of Ndu speakers was not an orderly invasion; local groups fought each other quite as much as they fought any Arapesh they encountered. An ethnographer of the Abelam describes the movement as the "jostling together of large, fairly densely packed Abelam villages, fighting each other and gradually moving as a whole in a northerly and later westerly direction" (Forge 1966: 24).[4] Arapesh groups in their path were wiped out, absorbed into the surging, turbulent tide of Abelam advancement, or displaced northward or westward to sanctuaries beyond the perimeter of fighting.

Although we do not know precisely when Abelam incursions into the foothills–plains region began, we do know that they continued until very recent times. Based on Abelam living memory and confirmed by Australian patrol reports, Forge (ibid.) reports that, "up till the imposition of government control [c. late 1930s] this process was still going on, especially in the west of the Abelam area, where the Abelam . . . were pushing back the [Ilahita] Arapesh to the north. . . ." Even today, Abelam groups beyond the southeastern boundary of Arapesh territory have a reputation among Arapesh border villages as scruffy, scrappy thieves who will snatch your land the moment your guard is down. This contact had an enormous influence on the course of Ilahita social evolution – from that time, to the very present.

How things used to be

Our earliest documented description of how an earlier Ilahita Arapesh culture might have appeared comes from the writings of Margaret Mead (1935, 1938, 1947) about the Mountain Arapesh – a culture she made famous for their almost complete lack of warfare[5] and for their highly egalitarian relations between men and women, where both men and women behaved in a manner that by Western standards is "maternal" and nurturant. This lack of warfare is a clue as to why the Abelam, who, like their cultural cousins on the Sepik river, such as the Iatmul, are extremely warlike, successfully pushed their way into the upper plains and foothill region. The Abelam groups were larger than those they encountered; they were also better organized, in that the coordinating of ritual activities involved skills and collaborations that were easily transferred to the battlefield.

Limited in settlement size by their steep habitat, the Mountain Arapesh are organized into small hamlets occupied by only a few extended families. Alitoa, the location of Mead's field work, was the largest settlement in the area, and it had only eighty-seven residents (Mead 1938: 202). In the lower foothills, terrain conditions would have permitted larger communities; even today, visitors from the mountains to the north marvel with envy at the luxury of flatness enjoyed by Ilahita residents. Still, judging from settlement patterns among the Bumbita Arapesh (Leavitt 1989), who are Ilahita's western neighbors, and more distantly related peoples farther west in the Torricelli mountains and foothills (e.g. Lewis 1975; Mitchell 1978), settlements would not have exceeded 300 persons, and were usually much smaller than that. Subsistence would have depended less on yams, more on taro; yam ceremonialism, yam competition, and yam gigantism would not have existed, though yam cultivation itself probably did; and hunting, foraging, and sago production would have contributed more to the diet, relative to gardening, than they were to do during Ilahita's heyday.

Because of the small size of settlements, most marriages would have been contracted between separate communities; that is to say, marriage exchange would have been based on local exogamy. With smaller size and greater mobility, settlements would have divided and recombined fairly readily, with a corresponding dispersal of descent groups. Descent groups would not have been too important, anyway; for, as we know from studies of similar societies in New Guinea and elsewhere, an individual's social identity is defined more by direct ties of blood, marriage, and residence, than by membership in an entity as abstract as a non-localized, corporate descent group, such as a clan.

Corresponding with these social features, ritual life would have tended to be relatively small in scale: local "family" observances marking birth, puberty, marriage, and death; shamanic appeals to supernatural agencies to heal the sick or fertilize the plants and animals that are important to human life. These activities would have been nothing like the majestic cults of the Middle Sepik region, including those of the Abelam: great collective enterprises uniting large villages under the patronage of powerful ancestral spirits; men's cults of war and human sacrifice, predicated on ranked secrecy and female exclusion, generating magnificent, world-class works of ritual art and architecture. The vivid contrast in ritual practices between tribes of the Middle Sepik and those of the coastal mountains was remarked upon by Mead, with special reference to the radically different gender inflections. Speaking of those Middle Sepik peoples who grant men brutal authority over women and children, she writes:

> In some tribes, a woman who accidentally sees the *tamberan* [sic] is killed. The young boys are threatened with dire things that will happen to them at their initiation, and initiation becomes a sort of vicious hazing in which the older men revenge themselves upon recalcitrant boys and for the indignities that they themselves once suffered. . . . Secrecy, age and sex-hostility, fear and hazing, have shaped its formal pattern. *But the Arapesh*, although they share part of the formal pattern with their neighbours, have changed all the emphases. In a community where there is no hostility between men and women, and where the old men, far from resenting the waxing strength of the young men, find in it their greatest source of happiness, *a cult that stresses hate and punishment is out of place.* And so the mountain people have revised most of the major points. Where other peoples kill a woman who chances on the secrets, and go to war against a community that does not keep its women sufficiently in the dark, the Arapesh merely swear

the woman to secrecy, telling her that if she does not talk to others nothing will happen to her.

(1935: 67–8; emphasis added)

Mountain Arapesh liberalism extended even to allowing uninitiated youths to participate in cult feasts. But, Mead continues, "if critical and orthodox strangers . . . are present, the uninitiated boys are hustled out of sight, for the Arapesh are sensitive about their own happily muddled unorthodoxy" (1935: 68).

Ilahita's special situation

In stark contrast with the Mountain Arapesh and other Torricelli groups, most of which were remote from Abelam influences, the Ilahita Arapesh became, in a word, "Abelamized." Not only did they embrace the Abelam cult that "stresses hate and punishment," they think of themselves as the original and most orthodox practitioners of it. There can be no doubt, however, that the Tambaran was adopted from the Abelam,[6] who, according to Forge (pers. comm.), were privately astonished at the zeal and literalness with which the Ilahita adopted and implemented these severe ritual practices. Along with this important ritual importation came many other changes which propelled Ilahita along a course of sociocultural evolution that made it almost unrecognizable as a descendant of the ancestral culture. The key to this development was the sudden increase in the size of these Arapesh villages, Ilahita in particular.

Whereas in the central area of their expansion the Abelam overcame whatever resistance they encountered, toward the northwest their way became blocked by the large and densely settled villages of the Ilahita Arapesh. Ironically, those communities were indirectly the creation of the Abelam themselves, who, as noted, had been shunting weaker peoples northward for generations. Their numbers swelled the ranks of the hamlets with which they took refuge, until, by the late nineteenth century, an equilibrium was reached whereby the new villages were a defensive match for the Abelam intruders.

An important point is that many of these refugees were, themselves, Abelam, or other Ndu speakers, such as the Kwanga, who were also under pressure from the Abelam (Map 2). In Ilahita village, several clans claim descent from Abelam who fled from fighting in the south; one of the six residential wards of Ilahita (see Chapter 5) claims to have arrived *en masse* as Kwanga-speaking refugees; another ward is an amalgam of Abelam and other units, who received sanctuary in Ilahita during the same period of intense fighting in the south. Two other groups – one Arapesh-speaking,

Plate 21 Armed warriors from a different village arrive at the ritual precinct. The mock aggression performed when friend and enemy villages join together in cult events is a reminder of the Tambaran's traditionally important role in the ideology and conduct of warfare.

Plate 22 A man of the Nggwal Bunafunei grade prepares to lie across the path of a group of men from an Abelam village, who are bringing a statue to contribute to Ilahita's forthcoming initiation ceremony. The gesture is commonly used to indicate gratitude to the visitors and praise of their donation.

the other Kwanga-speaking – were granted protection, and were established as independent villages on lands Ilahita seized from its (Arapesh) enemies. To this day these villages pay formal (albeit largely symbolic) tribute to Ilahita as their "mother," who fed and sheltered them in their time of need. Ilahita's acceptance of these displaced groups depended on its having room for expansion: available habitation sites, garden lands, sago groves, and hunting reserves, or resources that could be developed for these purposes. As Map 3 indicates, generations after the incorporation of these foreigners, Ilahita is still not crowded on the north and west. But if expansion room was a *necessary* condition for Ilahita's behavior, it was not a *sufficient* condition. A reason was needed, a strategic plan, for Ilahita leaders to grant hospitality, rather than simply send the refugees on their way, as the border villages did. The reason was that Ilahita was buffered from direct Abelam contact by those Arapesh border villages, four of which were Ilahita's traditional enemies. *Those* villages, not Ilahita, were being pressured and encroached upon. As refugees arrived, those villages had neither the resources nor the will to harbor them.

Ilahita had both the resources and the will, and it perceived that additional loyal fighting men would help them to dominate old enemies to the south.[7] Some of the refugees, as noted, were added to the main village. Others were given land that Ilahita did not own, could not conveniently use, or did not want. Indebted outsiders were strategically placed to enlarge Ilahita's security zone, to establish occupancy of recently conquered, peripheral territories, or to interfere with lines of communication between enemy villages. More than that, Ilahita established alliances with *Abelam* villages, with the object of pressuring their common enemies in a pincer movement. The incorporation of Abelam refugees and the strategic alliances with Abelam villages were the channels through which Abelam customs entered into and transformed Ilahita society.[8]

Within a short period of time – little more than a generation, it would seem – Ilahita village became a veritable powerhouse of cultural creativity, social engineering, and military effectiveness. It is impossible to exaggerate the importance of sheer population size in fostering this social and cultural vitality (Harris 1977; Johnson and Earle 1987). In all communities, *events* often precipitate collective performances: births, deaths, marriages, fights, arguments, scandals, visitations, etc. In a village the size of Ilahita, these were not rare or occasional happenings: they occurred with very great frequency, conferring a hum of sociocultural vibrancy on the place, and sustaining a this-is-where-the-action's-at aura that was the envy of visitors from other villages. By whatever criteria one measures social success, Ilahita had it. But all of these gains carried a cost – a cost that eventually, a century or so later, was to become unbearable. As Karl Marx might have put it, Ilahita's success carried with it the seeds of its own destruction.

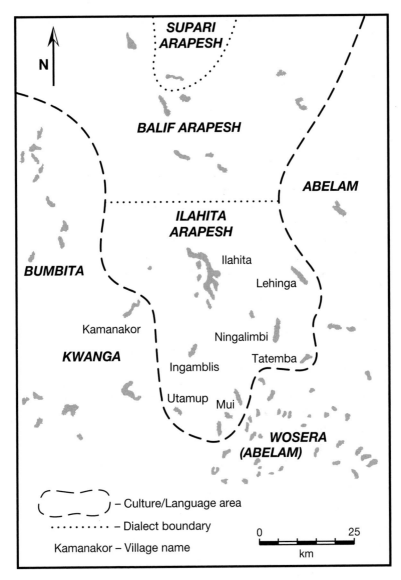

Map 3 Language-culture areas of Ilahita and its environs

A moral dilemma

Recall Margaret Mead's characterization of gender egalitarianism and paternal nurturance among the Mountain Arapesh. In domestic life, the people of Ilahita manifest similar values. If, in advance, one knew only of the violent, misogynistic rhetoric of the Tambaran, and of the sadistic hazing inflicted on young boys, one would not be prepared for the considerable tenderness and concern that men actually display towards wives and children in everyday life. When, in 1971, Margaret Mead visited Beverly and me in Ilahita and remarked that the place looked different but "felt" the same as her Mountain Arapesh of forty years earlier, it was this aspect of gentleness she was referring to. By adopting and intensifying the Tambaran, then, the men committed themselves to a world of two diametrically opposed value systems: the Tambaran, which demanded the ritual tormenting of youths and the radical degradation and exclusion of women in public affairs, as against an older tradition enjoining men to be nurturant and protective toward their wives and children (Tuzin 1982).

The moral dilemma that arose from this contradiction showed itself in various ways. Here is an example taken from mortuary customs. On the evening of a funeral, the immediate family of the deceased gathers in the home hamlet to perform a touching, rather eerie ceremony. Members of the family station themselves around the periphery of the clearing. Two or three of the men blow dirge-like blasts on conch-shell horns; then, the others call the name of the deceased into the surrounding forest. They listen. If no response is heard, they repeat the procedure, several times if necessary. In every observed case, someone eventually "hears" "*Mwein?*" ("What?") shouted back faintly, as if from a great distance, from the forest depths. This response is received with quiet joy and great relief; for it signifies that the deceased does not blame those present for his or her death, or nurse any ill will toward them from the grave. The joy and relief are much greater when the deceased is a woman of the family – a wife and a mother who now has the ghostly awareness that she had been victimized all her life by the Tambaran's deceptions and by her husband's complicity in them, but who, by her spectral "Mwein?," shows that she has forgiven him. Pitiful it is to see sorrow and fear overtake a man when his wife dies, even more so if they have been married for many years and there are accordingly many grievances to be forgiven.

As another indication of moral unease, men often risk Tambaran displeasure by secreting a piece of meat from a ritual feast and giving it discreetly to their wives. The wives are told that the Tambaran had eaten its fill and kicked aside this morsel, growling that it could be given to the women. The explanation stresses the separation of men and women, but the gift of food represents, in context, a kindness. Such mitigating acts, which contravene public (Tambaran) ideology, are an instance of what the sociologist Georg Simmel describes in his classic treatise on secrecy:

> For however destructive [a secret] often is for a relation between two if one of them has committed a fault against the other of which both are conscious, it can, on the contrary, be very useful for the relation if the guilty one alone knows of the fault. For, this causes in him a considerateness, a delicacy, a secret wish to make up for it, a yieldingness and selflessness, none of which could ever occur to him had he a completely untroubled conscience.
>
> (1950: 330 n.)

Near the end of my first field work, knowing of the men's moral contradiction, I asked a savvy cult elder why, in fact, women were excluded from the Tambaran. "After all," I remarked, "in Africa men have their cults and women have theirs, and in some places men and women have cults together. What would be the harm if you let the women share in the Tambaran?" The old gentleman thought for a moment. "Yes, it is true that sometimes men feel ashamed and guilty over eating good food while their wives go hungry. But if we told them now," he replied softly, "that for all these generations they have been deceived, they would make life unbearable for us. There is nothing we can do." As we are about to see, there *was* something they could do; and eventually, long after my friend was dead, they did it.

Mythic prophecy

Contact with the Abelam propelled Ilahita on an exciting course of development quite divergent from that of other Torricelli groups, including other Arapesh-speakers. But if Ilahita took maximum advantage of the opportunities afforded by that historical event, and flourished as a village because of it, their doing so was not without cost. As we have just seen, the incorporation and local development of the Tambaran generated a serious moral contradiction between the demands of ritual practice and the ancient, more benign impulses men felt toward their wives and children. Interestingly, the guilt and associated vulnerability of male legitimacy were projected and enshrined in a story that was independently imported during the same period that Abelam influences were being introduced.[9]

Despite its relatively recent arrival (1870's?), the story is a creation myth, an account of how people – not just the Ilahita, but *all* people – came to be. It was told to me on my very first day of field work, many years ago, by a group of villagers who declared that if my object was to understand their ways, then this is a story I must know; for this is where they came from, this is what they *are*. It is a tale of mystery, enchantment, and prophecy. And although I previously warned that myths cannot be taken as historically true, there are truths other than historical. This story is embedded in history but also transcends that history and is truthful of the Ilahita in its own fashion. As an 8-year-old girl of my acquaintance once replied when I asked if she knew what a "myth" was, "A myth is a story that is false on the outside, and true on the inside." So it is with "Nambweapa'w."

The story of Nambweapa'w

> The First Man is walking along when he hears the unusual sound of laughter coming from nearby. He goes to investigate and, from hiding, espies a group of cassowaries bathing in a pond (see Map 4, p. 73). Having removed their skins, they have become beautiful (human) women. The man secretly steals the skin of the one he most fancies, so that later, when the cassowary-women emerge to resume their skins, the one he has chosen cannot find hers. This leads to the man's taking her home with him, where he tricks her into piercing herself to create her external genitalia. They begin their married lives together. Her name is Nambweapa'w.
>
> Man and wife advance to old age producing a long line of alternately-sexed children, who later in the story intermarry and become the ancestral parents of all the world's peoples. The first-born, a son, is the ancestor of the Ilahita Arapesh. In an alternating pattern, the father takes the older children to the garden, while the mother stays home to care for the youngest; then, the next day, the parents reverse roles.
>
> The youngest child, also a son, is about 6 years old when he discovers that his father keeps a cassowary skin in hiding. He realizes this after the father has donned the skin a few times to frighten the youngster into ceasing his crying and whining. The next day, in exchange for some coconut tidbits which the boy cries for during meal preparation, he reveals this secret to his mother, who reacts by putting on the cassowary skin and running back to her natural home in the forest. Before finally leaving, however, she instructs her children on how they are later to join her in an area of grassfields, where she will be at that time.
>
> Accordingly, after some months they follow her, taking their old father with them. They hide him under a taro leaf at the prearranged

meeting place. Boys and girls climb into separate trees, with the oldest near the bottom, continuing upward in birth order, until the youngest is at the top. Starting with the oldest, each boy in turn blows a conch shell in the direction of the grassfields and then throws a grass spear. Each projectile goes a little farther than the previous one. Finally, that of the youngest soars much higher and farther, until it lands in a ground-crab hole right next to where Nambweapa'w is sitting, making vegetal salt.

Following the trail of grass spears, Nambweapa'w goes to her children. After ordering them down from the trees, she tells her sons to take up their spears so that they and their sisters can come with her. She notices that there is one unclaimed spear remaining, which she identifies as belonging to her husband. She demands to know where he is. The children, fearing for their father, do not tell her – until she threatens to kill them, whereupon they point to his hiding place. Finding him crouched under the taro leaf, Nambweapa'w uses his own spear to crush his head.

From there the story follows a course which recounts the creation of certain cultural and institutional forms: menstrual houses and Tambaran houses; and marriage – in this instance, between adjacent brothers and sisters, with Nambweapa'w taking the youngest, who is without a sister to marry, for herself. After a time, Nambweapa'w decides that it would not be good for their descendants all to speak the same language. Accordingly, she sends the boys up a betel palm, in birth order, with the oldest at the bottom. She then calls to them to come down. As each alights on the ground he is bitten by a certain kind of insect, causing each son in turn to speak a different language. The oldest speaks the language of Ilahita, while the remaining sons speak languages progressively farther afield. When the youngest reaches the ground he speaks a language utterly different from the others, a language that is now known to have been English.

Nambweapa'w's magic provides effortless abundance, a life in which death and pain and sorcery are unknown. This blissful existence is lost, however, when her children – all but the youngest – fecklessly violate the one food taboo she has imposed. She punishes them by turning herself into a wallaby and tricking the innocent, youngest son into killing her with a spear. Before she dies, she revokes her sustaining magic and ordains that life hereafter will have pain and drudgery and death. The youngest son scolds his siblings. In a blaze of moral indignation, he is swept away by a sudden flood – to America, "as we now know," where he fathers the white race, and from whence he will someday return, bringing the magic that was lost so long ago.

Myth and reality came together in September 1984. About a hundred years after "stealing" it, the men of Ilahita, metaphorically speaking, returned the "cassowary skin" to its rightful owner, and with it the power and autonomy that had always been secretly, naturally, hers. Just as, in the story, the revelation of the skin signified for Nambweapa'w that she had been tricked and that her (human) existence was based on masculine deceit, so in telling the women that the many Tambaran claims were lies and hoaxes, the men were admitting that the women's ritual subordination was nothing more than bondage, that they had all along been tricked into believing that the spirits were as real, powerful, and hateful toward them as the men said they were. Bravely, perhaps recklessly, the men had taken history into their own hands, obliterating a past in the hope of clearing the way to a glorious future. Under terms proclaimed by a strange Christian conversion move-ment ("the Revival") sweeping the region, the eradication of "Satanic" traditions, such as the Tambaran, would bring about a new age, a heaven-on-earth benignly governed by God, Jesus and the Holy Spirit, an idyll featuring many spiritual and material comforts.

Things did not go as expected. This is not the place to describe the women's revenge and the wholesale collapse of customs that ensued in the

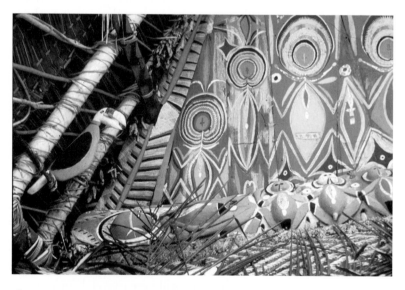

Plate 23 Detail of the façade of a Nggwal Bunafunei spirit house. The carved lintel (bottom) is an effigy of the First Man from the "Nambweapa'w" story, along with some of his and the Cassowary-Mother's alternately-sexed children. At the other end of the lintel (not shown) is Nambweapa'w herself, similarly carved and positioned.

aftermath of the revelation (see Tuzin 1997). Suffice it to say, in their act the men catastrophically terminated an adaptation that had served Ilahita magnificently for a hundred years, but had outlived its time and setting. Yes, that adaptation had serious costs: the labor and material resources expended on cult activities, and the hardships inflicted upon women and initiates. In some ways the Tambaran was brutal, but so were the conditions under which it emerged. Ultimately, the Tambaran was unsustainable; but, in its day, it displayed a functional efficiency sufficient for Ilahita to become one of the largest, most remarkable villages in the entire country.

We turn now to examine the structures and processes of Ilahita's adaptation. In doing so, let us not forget the importance of *warfare* in a nexus that includes a rising village population and increasing societal scale and complexity. The great Harvard psychologist William James once wrote that warfare is "the gory nurse that trained societies to cohesiveness"[10] (1911: 272; cf. Harrison 1993: 144). He could have been speaking of the Tambaran. And when that gory nurse faltered and eventually died, it took with it the very reason for Ilahita's continuance as the huge, integrated village it once was.

5   Residence structures

The challenge of living together

To those who live their lives in urban industrial society, a village of 1,500 persons may not seem very large or impressive. One or two high-rise apartment buildings could accommodate that number; a couple of downtown city blocks would be more than enough. Ilahita's achievement must be judged, therefore, in terms of the New Guinea context. Why should we do this? Why should we care about Ilahita at all? Because there is much we take for granted about large-scale sociality, and much that is obscured amid the incredible complexities and interdependencies of modern life.[1] If we are to understand the nature of social order, then it behooves our project to observe societal phenomena in a simpler, more visible setting.

Let us also adopt a proper sense of wonder at it all. Behind the crowd at every soccer match and every rock concert, behind the bustle in Times Square and the dignified proceedings of the Supreme Court, behind even the event of a university lecture – behind *all* human interactions that feature or imply cooperation among persons unknown to each other – lie millions of years of evolution during which such orderliness, on such a societal scale, would have been unthinkable. The wonder is not that soccer fans or concert enthusiasts are sometimes trampled, or that violence occasionally erupts on street corners; the wonder is that mayhem, murder, rape, and pillage are not ubiquitous!

With dismal frequency, humans show themselves to be extremely violent primates. Given the many recurrences of human aggression, perpetrated by both individuals and collectivities, it would appear that the genetic basis for this tendency has remained essentially unchanged since our species began. Early towns and cities did not come about because human nature suddenly became gentler or more xenophilic. They arose because innovations in culture, society, and, as a quasi-independent factor, technology, enabled or forced social relationships to extend beyond the narrow compass of kinship, wherein emotional attachments and the "axiom of amity" (Fortes 1969) generally kept family members from killing each other. People learned to live together not because our violent nature was repealed, but because structures emerged that enabled primitive impulses of a ghastly sort to be suppressed or channeled (Harrison 1993: 4). The case of Ilahita is an instructive instance of how, within a relatively short span of time, people who once lived apart managed to live together. And although this case has many singular features, we may be sure that some of the processes this village has undergone have occurred many times in human history.

As told early in this account, word of Ilahita's large size was what originally attracted me to studying that village. During the 1960s, at the time I was preparing for field work, area specialists were discussing why New Guinea settlements tended to be quite small (e.g. Lepervanche 1967/8; see also Hogbin and Wedgwood 1953/4; Forge 1972a). While it was true that some coastal and lowland riverine areas supported villages of a thousand or so inhabitants, everywhere else concentrations of such magnitude were virtually non-existent. The maximum size seemed to be 300, or about 80 adult males, beyond which settlements would almost invariably come apart; in many regions, settlement sizes never even approached 300.

What prevented settlements from exceeding the "magic number" of 300? Various explanations were proposed. The carrying capacity of the land, under conditions of hunting, foraging, and slash-and-burn agriculture, was certainly a limiting factor in many areas. A cognitive factor, suggested by studies of modern military organization, may be the inability of more than eighty men to know each other well and to cooperate effectively, especially as a fighting unit. Another common factor is the disruptive fear of destructive magic. Once established, sorcery and witchcraft beliefs put a strain on residential cohesion by making every misfortune, great and small, a product of one's neighbor's secret hostility. These factors may all be at work, but perhaps the best explanation is that the "big man" system of leadership is unable to integrate more than a modest number of individuals. Without hereditary rank and wealth, without stable judicial and police mechanisms for discouraging disruptive, divisive behavior, and with the rules of the political game allowing actors to shift allegiances fairly readily, local communities are never very secure in their integration. This is even truer in hunting societies (in New Guinea and elsewhere) than in horticultural societies. There, discord rarely escalates to a serious level; for, at the first sign of trouble, opponents can and do simply pick up their few belongings and leave (Feil 1987: 64; Marcus and Flannery 1996: 73); hence the tendency of such groups to be less war-like than those that are less mobile.[2]

Against this prevalence of small-size settlements in New Guinea, Ilahita is anomalous and provocative. My preparatory reading had led me to expect to find a super-bigmanship, or an emergent chiefship, but that was not to be. If anything, leaders were less visible in Ilahita than in many other New Guinea places. Here was a society that labored under all the restrictions found elsewhere, and yet produced a village five times the theoretical maximum. Other settlements in the region, it is true, also exceed that maximum: villages of many hundreds, even as many as a thousand inhabitants, are not unheard of in the Sepik area. Their enabling social mechanisms are not dissimilar in kind from those found in Ilahita, which is what gives the Sepik area its distinctive sociocultural flavor. The difference is, Ilahita's social system is far more elaborate than that found anywhere else. That elaborateness is related to Ilahita's large size, as both cause and effect.

Hamlets

Ilahita is built on a series of ridgetops, radiating spiderlike from a central hub (Map 4). Strung out along the lines of the ridges are eighty-three named hamlets. These are the primary residential units, the grassroots of village life; indeed, until serious cash-cropping in the late 1960s gave new economic autonomy to the nuclear family, hamlets were often tantamount to domestic units.[3] A typical hamlet consists of a densely packed circle of dwelling and yam-storage houses. These structures are built on the ground with an A-frame design, roofed portico, and sago-thatch walls, facing on to a central clearing. Some hamlets contain an open-sided pavilion where resident men enjoy casual get-togethers over tobacco and betel nut, and where overnight visitors sleep – in watchful view of the residents. One might also find small dormitories built by and for adolescent girls and boys, respectively, with the former occasionally used by young married women during menstrual periods.[4]

Hamlets vary in social composition but generally feature one or two (rarely more) patrilines,[5] the adult males of which individually own the carefully demarcated house sites. Because post-marital residence is conventionally virilocal ("in the husband's place"), the social structure of a typical hamlet centers on a small group of brothers and/or the sons of brothers, their families, married sons and their families, and aged parents. It is not unusual for a married daughter to be in residence, at least temporarily, to help her parents during peak gardening periods, to assist in the care of sick or enfeebled family members, or to obtain temporary relief from a difficult marriage situation. Sometimes, too, a married daughter might induce her husband to reside uxorilocally ("in the wife's place") for a time, because her

Plate 24 Five-year-old Alex Tuzin plays in the hamlet clearing during a rainstorm. Note the house form and, in the background, smoke from a cooking fire rising through another house's sago thatch. Part of the mythic stone of Baingap (Tuzin 1997: 138) is shown on the left.

natal family needs their help, because relations are strained between her and the other women of his hamlet, or because they have been given temporary use of gardening plots belonging to her natal group. Adult sons of out-marrying sisters of the group are sometimes in residence, resulting from an unrequited marriage exchange in the preceding generation. This occurs if, in the preceding generation, a man received a wife without giving a sister in exchange, and therefore must later yield one of his children in adoption to the wife's group (see below).

Although dwelling houses contain hearths and are occupied by nuclear families, most daily activity goes on in the hamlet clearing or, during inclement weather, under the sheltered porticoes. On clear, moonlit nights many prefer to sleep on mats in the clearing, at least until the chill of the small hours drives them indoors. Relations within the hamlet are marked by a casual, more or less constant, sharing of goods and services. A family returning home late from the gardens can expect to be offered soup from another's pot while their own food is cooking. Garden work, house-building, child care, tool use and manufacture – mutual assistance of these sorts, though not restricted to the hamlet group, is definitely clustered there. Some outsiders inevitably belong to this collaborative sphere, but by virtue of personal kin or friendship ties, rather than because of their hamlet affiliation.

Structurally speaking, hamlets exist in themselves and do not interact, as such, with other hamlets.[6] No overarching social structure binds hamlets into the larger community, and in theory any hamlet could pick up and leave the village without injury to higher-level structural relationships. In traditional practice, however, this would not happen, which is why structures to prevent it from happening would be (1) redundant, because dense, overlapping ties of kinship, marriage, and other forms of exchange already tightly bind *members* of the hamlet, *qua* individuals, to many persons in other hamlets; (2) unworkable, because their rigidities would impede local inter-hamlet residence shifts of an innocuous or stress-alleviating (and therefore socially positive) sort; and (3) unnecessary, since, under traditional circumstances, it was known that a hamlet-size group striking off on its own would be annihilated by (village-sized) enemy neighbors ready to pounce on it. Autonomous, hamlet-size groups might be the norm for hunter-gatherer cultures, or for terrain-limited cultures such as the Mountain Arapesh; but once village organization became established among the Ilahita Arapesh, unattached hamlets were no longer viable.[7]

In a constructive sense, Ilahita hamlet groups are free to expand, contract, relocate or disband altogether, without jeopardizing village social structure or the wider social relationships of their members. Like the spacers of a cement bridge that allow for expansion and contraction, lest temperature changes cause the structure to crack, the flexibility of hamlets contributes to the integrity of village social structure. By the same token, under conditions of pronounced change in the social environment – to wit, the cessation of warfare – this freedom of movement at the hamlet level comes to impart a grassroots vulnerability to the village's spatial (and therefore social) integration.

The physical boundary of the hamlet may not always be obvious to the casual observer, but resident dogs, pigs, and roosters will chase intruders precisely to it and no farther; toddlers will not stray beyond it unaccompanied; and adults returning heavily laden from the garden will, upon crossing it, noticeably relax their pace and begin to ease the burden from off their head or shoulder. Outsiders passing through the hamlet (as they often must, given the generally linear arrangement of the hamlets along the ridge) are expected to be about their business, and any loitering is an immediate cause for suspicion or challenge. From a residential standpoint, then, the hamlet is the fundamental social and psychological unit. It is the place of security, acceptance, comfort, and familiarity – in a word, it is home.

If the amity of hamlet life is grounded in the intimacy of the social setting, so is the discord. The same understandings which, for example, expect brothers to be affectionate, supportive, and generous, provoke a sense of betrayal and moral indignation when things go wrong. In some cases brothers simply do not get along well together: chronic rivalries or dislikes, perhaps dating from childhood, may lie in wait for some trivial incident to set them off and lead to residential separation. More commonly, trouble in the hamlet begins as a marital dispute or as a dispute among women. Responsible co-residents may attempt to arbitrate or remain neutral, but when (as often happens) their efforts fail they may find themselves in bitter opposition to their siblings or parents. Polygynous ("multiple wives") households, especially those in which the husband is young and inexperienced, are proverbially unsettled by co-wifely rivalries which often lead to wider disruptions. Even a fight among small children may, under the right circumstances, bring the adults of the hamlet into the fray.

Human nature being what it is, one may safely assume that domestic strife of this kind has always been a feature of hamlet life; Ilahita's integrative success is by no means attributable to folks being more neighborly than elsewhere. Under the conditions that prevailed prior to the cessation of chronic warfare (c. 1952), however, there were powerful incentives for disputes to be managed without recourse to residential separation. Practically speaking, there were not many places for disaffected residents to go. With a village endogamy rate of 93 percent, few men had relatives in other villages with whom they could take up residence; endemic warfare made the prospect of setting up camp in the bush unacceptably dangerous; and a man moving in with his mother's or wife's family of origin would risk losing legal rights and identities that require active participation in the affairs of his agnatic group.

The cessation of warfare eventually caused the fabric of village integration to begin to unravel. With the danger of warfare removed, hamlet-sized groups had the option of moving to locations outside the main village, sites that had often been World War II refuges, where coconuts planted then were now grown to maturity. By the mid-1980s, following the decline in ritual activity and authority by cult elders, and the rise of competing interests, such as cash-cropping, residential dispersal out of the main village was very advanced. It was as though Ilahita were drifting toward a residence structure reminiscent of the one that prevailed before its stupendous growth and "urban" development, before the Abelam arrived on the scene. For present purposes, the relevant point is that the fluidity of hamlet composition helped to sustain Ilahita during its heyday, because it relieved local stresses while neither undermining the higher-level structures of village integration, nor resulting in the departure of individuals and small groups from the village.

At this level of organization, there is nothing special about Ilahita; the description would apply equally well to most New Guinea villages, certainly most villages in the Sepik region. At higher structural levels, though, Ilahita starts to look special.

Wards

In the early Australian patrol reports one sometimes sees Ilahita referred to as a "confederation" of villages, rather than as the ritually unified, single village it is.[8] This misperception was caused partly by the unprecedented size of the village, and partly by the fact that Ilahita is composed of six semi-autonomous residential sectors, which I call "wards." Each ward is named, each occupies its own territorial section of the village, and each is large enough to be an independent village in its own right. These wards are listed in Table 1.

Plate 25 Aerial view of Ililip ward, indicating the linear arrangement of hamlets along the ridgetop. The two "legs" meet (center) at the main ceremonial plaza of the ward. Part of Hengwanif ward can be seen stretching across the top of the picture; Balanga and Bwi'ingili (not shown) are off the picture at the left and top, respectively.

The disparity in ward sizes is mitigated by the fact that substantial portions of the Ililip and Balanga populations inhabit large, permanent settlements outside of the main village, which were established under warfare circumstances mentioned in Chapter 4.[9] Removing them from the totals would bring the figures for Ililip and Balanga in line with those of the other wards, implying that the perceived sizes of wards in the main village are about the same.

Table 1 Ilahita ward populations, 1969

Ward	Population
Balanga	309
Bwi'ingili	172
Hengwanif	148
Ilifalemb	213
Ililip	487
Nangup	161
TOTAL	1,490

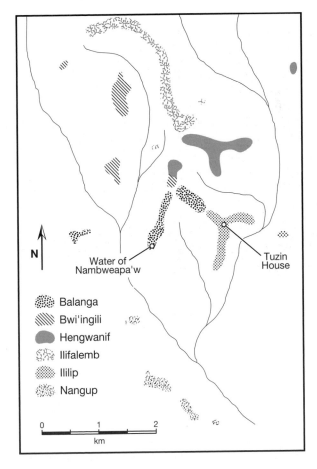

Map 4 Ilahita village

Of the six wards, four of them (Balanga, Bwi'ingili, Hengwanif, and Ililip) are very ancient; the Ilahitans maintain they have been there since the village began, around the mythic time of Nambweapa'w. The other two wards were formed in the nineteenth century by refugees from the fighting to the south and southeast (Chapter 4): Ilifalemb was stitched together from remnants of Abelam and Arapesh groups; Nangup was added *en masse* from the direction of the Ndu-speaking Kwanga, who, likewise, had been pressured by the Abelam.

Although a ward is composed of a dozen or more residential hamlets, socially and ritually it is more than their sum; in other words, wards are more than merely residential sectors. To begin with, wards are composed of patriclans the constituents of which are the unnamed, genealogically shallow patrilines dispersed among the ward's hamlets. Clans have no jurisdiction outside their home ward, though different clans of the same *name* do occur in different wards.

One does not have to live long in the village to realize that each ward has its own "personality": subtle differences in language pronunciation and in fashions concerning, say, food varieties and body-ornamentation details exist between them. These are aspects of a general differentiation that is sometimes rivalrous. Young men from different wards occasionally get into fistfights, often as a result of gratuitous insults or when one side appears too boldly interested in the other's sisters. Because ward boundaries extend into the surrounding bush and garden lands, where privacy is obtainable, adulterous liaisons (or suspicions thereof) are a common source of inter-ward conflict. Finally, a ward's external relations are its own: aggressive raiding is typically directed at a ward's particular external enemies, whereas assistance from one or more other wards is expected only in defensive circumstances. Such a pattern has been reported elsewhere in the Sepik region (Harrison 1993: 66).

The distinctiveness of interests and character among the several wards is sustained, also, by the relative infrequency of intermarriage, through which homogenizing influences might otherwise circulate. Echoing Ilahita's high rate of endogamy (93 percent), marriage transactions tend to occur within the ward, to which extent *village* integration is not served, and the wards do indeed come to resemble a cluster of confederated villages. A census taken in 1969–70 yields the percentages of ward endogamy shown in Table 2 (see also Tuzin 1976: 93). In each case, the incidence is much higher than it would be (i.e. 17 percent) if marriage contracts were randomly distributed in the village.

That the highest rates shown are in the non-indigenous wards of Ilifalemb and Nangup, indicates that they have yet to assimilate fully to the village since being formed from refugee groups late in the nineteenth

Table 2 Ward endogamy rates, 1969

	%
Balanga	45
Bwi'ingili	38
Hengwanif	49
Ilifalemb	79
Ililip	69
Nangup	73

century. Ililip's elevated rate of endogamy, on the other hand, is permitted by its very large size and the corresponding abundance of marriage partners available there.

At this juncture the attentive reader might ask, if Ilahita's hamlets are too small to make it on their own in a dangerous world, what about the wards? We have seen that in size, sub-cultural "personality," and residential separateness, the wards are close to being villages already; indeed, by New Guinea standards, they could rate as rather large villages. In the event of dissension, what would prevent a disgruntled ward from leaving the village? At the very least, the boundaries between them – physical, social, and behavioral – would seem to be lines of serious potential cleavage. This is all quite true, and this is where the picture starts to get complicated.

Mechanical solidarity

In his important work *Division of Labor in Society* (1893), French sociologist Emile Durkheim distinguished two analytic types of social solidarity, or, in other words, alternative models for the way in which categories of persons are defined and systematically interact in comprising a social unity. *Organic* solidarity, which is most forcefully displayed by modern industrial society, is based on a differentiation in the division of labor. Like the physical organism which inspired this concept, different "organs" contribute different functions to the whole: the cobbler makes shoes, the miller grinds flour; each requires the products of the other. Projecting this across the wide welter of occupations, and the hierarchies into which many of them are organized, one can see that modern society is held together by myriad unlike exchanges supplying life's necessities and comforts.[10] By the same token, this elaborate system of interdependency implies that individuals and family groups are extremely lacking in self-sufficiency.

Ilahita and other segmentary societies manifest the type of solidarity Durkheim termed *mechanical*. This is characterized by uniformity and minimal differentiation in social and occupational structure.[11] The integrative hazards facing such a society are fairly obvious. Imagine a society in which each minimal social unit (say, the nuclear family) is not only structurally identical to every other, but is self-sufficient in food, clothing, shelter, defense, and every other essential. If families require nothing from each other, what would bind them together to make a larger society? The answer is, nothing; it would even be stretching the notion of "society" to apply it to such a congeries of minimal units.

As it happens, although many simple societies come close to approximating this description, none known to history or anthropology does so completely. However self-sufficient the minimal social unit in some societies may be, in no known society do such units supply their own marriage partners, and thus display *reproductive* self-sufficiency. "Again and again in the world's history," wrote Edward B. Tyler, the leading British anthropologist of his day, "savage tribes must have had plainly before their minds the simple practical alternative between marrying-out and being killed out" (1889: 29). Whatever the practical utility of not marrying within one's close kin group may be – and there are many other theories about the origins and persistence of this avoidance – it is a fact that exchanging marriage partners is the most primordial, most universal way groups positively relate to one another. In situations of mechanical solidarity, this exchange may often come close to being the *only* structure of inter-group integration. In other, more elaborate situations marriage remains the starting point of other interactions pursued between the transacting groups: mutual assistance, ceremonial exchanges of food and services, and the many day-to-day reciprocities among the network of kin created by the marriage. This is what we call society; and in a mechanically ordered society, it is the marriage exchange that starts it all.

The relevance of marriage exchange to Durkheim's concept of mechanical solidarity is that it is the classic instance of the practice of exchanging like for like (e.g. Lévi-Strauss 1969). In principle one could argue that, ubiquitous though it is, this interdependency is unnecessary; brothers and sisters could save themselves a lot of trouble simply by marrying each other – a common enough occurrence in myths of creation. Why, then, do groups seek marriage partners elsewhere? Much folklore and, again, many scientific theories purport to explain why systematic incest is not a good idea, at least in the long run. But other sorts of like-for-like exchanges are hardly intelligible to the theorist, except as a mechanism for promoting interdependency *for its own sake*, or for the sake of secondary benefits based on that contrived interdependency. The Ilahita exchanges of yams for yams, and pigs for pigs, are socially motivated in this way (cf. Rubel and Rosman 1978; Weiner 1992).

Even more so – in the sense that it is more perfectly motivated by social and symbolic rather than practical considerations – is the system of reciprocal men's cult initiation practiced by the Ilahita and other Sepik societies. Thus, the men of Group A initiate the sons of Group B; then, years later, at the next turn in the ritual cycle, the men of Group B initiate the sons of Group A. In Ilahita, this ritual interdependence is conceptualized as the simultaneous *sharing and exchanging* of a spirit entity ("tambaran") these two groups hold in common, which is embodied in paintings, sculptures, and other paraphernalia that are transferred at the moment of initiation. More than that, it is in the act of transmitting active ownership between the two partner groups that the cult spirit is realized, revivifying its power and infusing it into the partnership and its ritual works. One could not ask for a purer example of the Gift, the exchanges of which, according to Marcel Mauss (1925), are *morally-charged*, obligatory transactions that sustain highly personal relationships between individuals and groups. In this respect, gifts categorically differ from "commodities," which dominate urban socio-economic life, and which are exchanged in rational, instrumental, and impersonal transactions. In large measure, the making of the modern world was a shift in emphasis from gift-based exchange to commodity-based exchange.[12]

The following two chapters address the social structures and processes that enabled this large village to stay together for as long as it did. At times, the details will be dauntingly complex, even in the relatively simplified forms in which I have tried to present them. This is unavoidable, for it is the very intricacies of the system, propelled as they are by the logic of mechanical solidarity, that form the evolutionary link between population growth and expanding societal scale. While the details of this evolutionary matrix are unique to Ilahita, the observation that social structures adapt themselves to populations applies to all time and all places in human history. Let us see how, in the case of Ilahita, this was done.

6 The dual organization

Elementary structures

Although highly complex in detail, the Ilahita system is based on the simplest of all principles: the dual opposition of equivalent structures at each level in the organization. In such schemes, the two opposed structures are known by anthropologists as "moieties."[1] As a pure instance of mechanical solidarity, the system's complexity is formed geometrically, by progressive subdivisions, such that each moiety comes to contain *within itself* a lower-level moiety structure. Thus, a society divided into the moieties A and B becomes a step more complex when each moiety divides in half internally ("1" versus "2"), with the 1s and 2s forming the moieties A_1B_1 and $A_2 B_2$. These moieties are said to "crosscut" the A/B moieties, resulting in four possible combinations, or cells: A_1, A_2, B_1, B_2.[2] At the next stage, each of these four cells *itself* divides in half ($A_1x, A_1y, A_2x, A_2y, B_1x, B_1y, B_2x, B_2y$), with the 'x's and 'y's forming a set of moieties crosscutting *both* of the other moiety sets.[3] Note that, although each successive subdivision produces smaller cells, all of the moieties are ideally the same size, for each dual division crosscuts the *entire* society. This is a crucial feature, without which the successive subdivisions would describe a process of disintegration, rather than the ever more tightly integrated progression displayed by the Ilahita social system.

Continuing this process of subdividing and crosscutting, a process known as "structural involution," one would quickly produce a structure that is quantitatively very complex, and yet, because of the logic informing it, qualitatively very simple. Ilahita's system is composed of *eight* sets (or layers) of crosscutting moieties, making it the most elaborate dual organization ever documented.

This elaborateness carries over into the structuring of many ritual practices. Each set of moieties presides over a specific type of ritual activity (e.g. competitive pig hunting) or symbolic station (e.g. left and right in the spirit-house design). By this arrangement, the moiety sets remain functionally distinct from one another, even as they are interconnected as elements of the complex, unified framework of the Tambaran. The presence of such internal functional diversity might mistakenly be seen as a symptom of "organic" social solidarity. In fact, the system remains true to the "mechanical" type, in that the exchanging units are calculatedly alike. Thus, for example, instead of doctors and cobblers exchanging services and goods with each other (the "organic" mode), it would be as if doctors exchanged with doctors, and cobblers exchanged with cobblers, and yet *every* man was *both* a practitioner of medicine and a maker of shoes. The matter of which item – medical services or footware – was to be exchanged on a particular occasion was determined not by the presence of classes of occupational specialists, but by the ritual scheduling of particular kinds of exchange, in unending sequence.

The system's complexity directly reflects and enables village size. In the case of internal population growth, certain groups ("cells") in the dual organization may grow too large to work well together in performing their designated tasks (cf. Johnson 1982). Strains develop as the group increases to a certain critical point, whereupon it splits. This may trigger a corresponding split in their partner group in the opposite moiety, or the system may adjust itself in some other way. The reverse also occurs: if some cell in the dual organization is below minimum manpower to perform its ritual work, it may give up its autonomy and merge with another cell in the same moiety – again, causing its partner cell in the other moiety to adjust itself to this structural change. The point is that the system as a whole, by virtue of finely geared, easily deployed balancing mechanisms, is able to contract and expand in response to population changes, without affecting its general character or integrative efficiency. In the case of exogenous growth, as in the addition of refugee groups (Chapter 4), other adjustment mechanisms come into play, by way of preserving the symmetry of the village dual organization (see below).

In the preceding chapter, I used the example of marriage exchange to illustrate the dual-organization structure. In fact, many such systems – probably the great majority of them – are predicated on exogamous moieties, and the regulation of marriage is the principal function of the dual organization. Other functions may accrue to moieties, or moieties may be subdivided according to a more complex, longer cycling pattern of marriage exchange; but the structuring of marriage, in various forms, is so commonly a feature of dual organization, that anthropologists sometimes loosely treat moieties as exogamous by definition.

Ilahita's dual organization is somewhat unusual, therefore, in having no direct connection with marriage; instead, its reciprocities exist exclusively as the structural apparatus and ritual activities of the Tambaran, the men's cult. There is good circumstantial evidence, however, that Ilahita's dualistic model originated in the domain of marriage, and that in the course of social evolution these exchange structures became detached from marriage and were redeployed in the ritual sphere (Tuzin 1976: 135–48, 308–18). Marriage, so to speak, became "deregulated." As small, presumably exogamous groups joined together into sizeable villages, and the population of locally available marriage partners increased accordingly, convention ceased to dictate whom (or into what category) you must marry; rather, it merely defined the group into which you must *not* marry, and left the positive choice open. In anthropological terminology, this was a shift from a "prescriptive" to a "proscriptive" marriage system – another step in the making of the modern world.

As noted, the Ilahita dual organization has elaborated itself as the structural framework of the Tambaran, an institution which, above all, sanctifies the village as a spiritual unity. Spirit houses belonging to the two lowest grades may occur in each ward; but for each of the two highest grades, Nggwal Bunafunei and Nggwal Walipeine, respectively, all ritual activities are centered on a single, large house, which symbolizes the unification of all ritual dualities (see frontispiece). During the great ceremonial gatherings, the cult spirits belonging to the many clans, and transmitted through individual initiation partnerships between men belonging to opposite subclans, congregate in the house and are conceived of as a kind of parliament. When this "parliament" convenes, a higher spiritual unity is created. Just as the transmitting of a spirit (i.e. its paraphernalia) between individual partners re-creates that spirit as an active force, so on the collective level the simultaneous transmitting of the entire set of such spirits re-creates the spiritual totality that is the village. This alchemy occurs through the structure of the dual organization, which, at its highest, most inclusive level, unites one half of the village in complementary opposition to the other half. This leads us to the details of the dual organization.

Dual structures

Although Ilahita's dual organization consists of eight crosscutting moiety systems, for the purposes of this study I shall focus only on the three highest-level moiety systems: (1) village moieties, Laongol and Bandangel, which separate the wards (and by implication their constituent clans) into opposed halves at the village level; (2) ward moieties, Afa'afa'w and Ondondof, which divide each ward internally into dualistically opposed clan assemblages; and (3) initiation moieties, Sahopwas and Owapwas, which divide each clan into two opposed subclans.[4] Although subclans may participate as groups, most of the ritual work done at the level of the initiation moieties occurs between hereditary exchange partners who are individuals or patrilines belonging to the opposite subclans.[5]

In considering how these three moiety systems mutually interconnect, and in so doing serve the needs of village integration, it is important to know that each division spans the entire society. The organizing principle is: subdivide each part, and then reunite all like subparts along the new axis formed. Thus, each ward is divided into Afa'afa'w and Ondondof moieties, and on certain occasions all of the Afa'afa'w groups in Ilahita join against all of the Ondondof groups. Likewise, every clan is divided into Sahopwas and Owapwas moieties, and on certain occasions all of the Sahopwas groups in the village join against all of the Owapwas groups.

The total system is shown schematically in Figure 1, which depicts, through stepwise increments, the logic of its multiple layers and cross-connections. Figure 1(a) shows only the four primordial wards (the component circles)[6] of the village (the enclosing square), without regard to any structural relationship between them. In Figure 1(b), the village is shown to be divided, vertically, into the village moieties, each of which contains two wards. To this arrangement is added, in Figure 1(c), the fact that each ward is internally subdivided into ward moieties, and that, by implication, all of the shaded semicircles may be combined, over and against the combined unshaded semicircles. The triangles added in Figure 1(d) refer to constituent patriclans, which are themselves dualistically subdivided into subclans, shown as black and white. As with the ward moieties, the Figure implies that all of the black sub-triangles may be combined, over and against the combined white sub-triangles. Figure 1(e) adds to this array a fifth ward (Nangup), which joined the village in relatively recent times, and was integrated by being divided internally along coincident axes of village moiety and ward moiety oppositions, as in the manner shown. Finally, Figure 1(f) adds yet another ward (Ilifalemb) to the village, but without complete integration. As indicated, this ward maintains its own dual organization – its own Tambaran; the dashed lines represent the fact that in the decades following World War II, this ward became increasingly involved in the Tambaran of the main village, such that by the time of my field work (1969) its ritual independence had become somewhat vestigial (see below).

For the purposes of grasping the key to Ilahita's success as a village, it is worth mastering Figure 1, for it comes close to capturing the integrative genius of the dual organization. It will also prove useful as a guide during the remainder of this chapter.

82   *The dual organization*

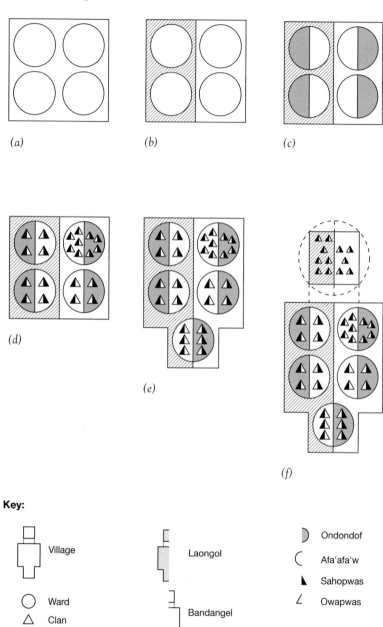

Figure 1 The Ilahita dual organization

The transparency of the system

Significantly, although the villagers are very aware of the various (named) components of the system, and can talk about individual dual structures in precise terms, they do not have a sense of the system as a whole, except insofar as they perceive the village to be a unitary entity symbolized in the person of the Tambaran. For example, not until I pointed it out to them did cult elders realize that clan names did not cross the village-moiety line. Nor do they recognize that the integrity of the village depends upon the workings of the dual organization; instead, they see social harmony, and the smooth interactions that constitute that harmony, as blessings of the Tambaran's spiritual patronage. If things go wrong, it is because relationships between men and the Tambaran are askew, implying that the remedy must come through ritual action.

From top to bottom, the dual organization is cast in ritual terms. In other words, although the dual organization operates in many arenas that we might consider "secular" – economic exchanges, political competitions, warfare, the dynamics of descent-group formation, etc. – to the people, the organization's intimate association with the Tambaran implies that all such arenas are imbued with ritual significance. However practical the actions taken in those arenas might be they are seen by the actors to be expressions or mandates of the Tambaran. The result is that virtually all of social life is suffused with spiritual meaning.

By the same token, the dazzle of Tambaran significance helps to obscure from actors the fact that the dual organization is an integrated totality composed of many structures and requiring constant adjustment. Perhaps this is for the best. Perhaps social systems work most smoothly when they are transparent, when there is an illusion of permanence and stability beyond human control; when the necessary tinkerings are not perceived as having aggregate structural effects, even though they are precisely the mechanism through which systems change and are sustained.

Furthermore, the uncognized nature of the overall system, whereby the actors look after the details and the system looks after itself, illustrates an important general feature of social evolution. The philosopher Sir Karl Popper sagely observes that the structure of our social environment arises, as a rule, out of "the indirect, the unintended and often the unwanted by-products" of decisions and actions taken by anonymous individuals according to the logic of their situation (1950: 93; cf. Flannery 1968: 85). "[E]ven most of the few institutions which were consciously and success-fully designed . . . do not turn out according to plan . . . because of the unintended social repercussions resulting from their intentional creation" (ibid.).[7] Once institutions are in place their existence and their effects become part of the "logic of the situation" presented to actors – but only in combination with other factors, many of which are historically or bio-graphically particular, and, as such, are accidental to the structure of the overall system. As in the case of biological evolution, although the overall movement of the system may appear to be directional, it is without intelligent purpose or design; in technical parlance, it is non-teleological.

Popper is speaking of social evolution in general. What he says is perhaps all the more true in pre-literate societies, where life's conventions are entirely mediated by living actors, without the benefit of written codes or written standards. Indeed, common sense confirms that social evolution can only occur as an emergent property of experience: the actions, percep-tions, and ideas of individuals in a collective, temporal setting (Marcus and Flannery 1996: 31). In the case of Ilahita, the organization's thorough-going dualistic character is the product of a mechanical form of solidarity, combined with the primordial, extremely adaptable practice of exchanging like for like. Without any modification, the dual principle inherent in reciprocal exchange between individuals can be applied to relationships of increasing inclusiveness, all the way to the very boundaries of the social universe. More than in any other form of organization, dualism enables any structured pairing to be a perfect miniature of the whole.

Village moieties

Starting at the top of the system, the paramount division of the village is that separating the two moieties. With the exception of Nangup and Ilifalemb (Figure 1) wards belong to one moiety or the other. The moiety names, Laongol and Bandangel, are not translatable, but in usage they convey the sense of "this and that." In Tambaran matters, and in quasi-ritual contexts such as funerals and yam competitions, the moieties are aggressively rivalrous. In fact, in Ilahita, ceremonial threat displays are markers of ritual interdependence, whether between groups or individuals featured in cult contexts. Between moieties, this mock aggression is enacted between groups which are also separate residential communities, namely, wards. Given that ward members are often suspicious of outsiders anyway, ritual antagonism tends to coincide with – and possibly reinforces – actual animosity.

In Ilahita the presence of six wards complicates the picture, and has produced more specific rivalries within the gross moiety opposition. Thus, Ililip and Balanga wards belong to opposite moieties and relate to each other in the aggressive manner prescribed. Similarly, Hengwanif and Bwi'ingili are principal antagonists. Nangup, upon its arrival in the nineteenth century, was split internally: integration into the system was

Plate 26 A cult elder listens intently to a colleague's speech during a Tambaran conclave. The flower arrangement in his hair signifies that he is of the Laongol village moiety.

achieved by opposing each Nangup half to *both* of the wards of the opposite moiety (Figure 1(e)). Between the two halves themselves, a form of dualistic opposition exists, which operates between groups as ward moieties – a relational field more benign than that between village moieties. Ilifalemb, the other refugee ward, did not join the main system at all, but formed its own organization and has its own, separate and somewhat differently styled, Tambaran (Figure 1(f)).[8]

Another twist added to the Ilahita system, one not found in other villages in the vicinity, is that wards of opposite moieties that are not directly antagonistic (e.g. Ililip and Hengwanif) view each other ambivalently as ritual "friends" and as go-betweens with the main "enemy" ward. Between wards of the same moiety (e.g. Ililip and Bwi'ingili) there is no ritual competition whatsoever. Table 3 arranges the wards according to moiety affiliation and constituent clans; arrows connect wards that are directly opposed at the moiety level of organization.

The table reveals two additional features. First, clan names occurring in more than one ward do not cross village-moiety lines. This separation imparts a descent aspect to the moieties, such that they could be seen as "super-clans." Also suggestive of this aspect is the fact that both clans and village moieties are *totemic*; that is, each is symbolically identified with a

Table 3 Ilahita village moieties, showing wards, clans, and membership size

LAONGOL (177)	BANDANGEL (215)
Hengwanif (53)	**Bwi'ingili** (54)
Owapwi	Balangapwi
Hengwanif	Indibi
Sahopwi	Eleputa
Afinga	Tata
	Ililip (134)
	Balangapwi I
Balanga (92)	Eleputa
Laongol	Indibi
Sahopwi	Tata
Owapwi	Atefin
Bundahimbil	Balangapwi II
	Mano'um
	Sao'um
	Afenim
Nangup (32)	**Nangup** (27)
Laongol	Balangapwi
Tatemba	Eleputa
Bundahimbil	Indibi

particular species of bird. Virtually wherever they are found – including in Arapesh clans – totems signify an essential identity among members of the reference group: a common nature usually attributed to descent from a common ancestor, who is often mythically portrayed as a member of the totemic species.[9] Although the Arapesh do not consciously view village moieties in such terms, the presence of descent-like elements does hint at the underlying logic, and perhaps even the history, of their construction. I will return to this point in a moment.

The second feature in Table 3 is that, comparing moiety oppositions with the ward locations shown on Map 4, it can be seen that the ritual relationships are intelligible also in spatial terms. The four wards are arranged in a square in which opposite corners are moiety partners, while adjacent corners are either "friends" or "enemies" (see also Figure 2, below). Previously I mentioned that boundary-sharing communities frequently suspect one another of nefarious acts. The pattern is mirrored by ritual oppositions within the village; and, with partner wards located at opposite corners, ritual allies share neither residential nor garden boundaries. Lacking this boundary tension, partner wards within the village moieties are better able to maintain the prescribed amity. In this way, appropriate spatial relations are significant contributors to the system's status quo.

Ward moieties

The clans of each ward are arranged into two groups, or "ward moieties," which are individually named but are also called by the generic names Afa'afa'w and Ondondof. The former name signifies "those who go first," and the latter, "those who come behind." This refers to complementary ritual statuses, by which Afa'afa'w initiates enter the spirit house ahead of Ondondof initiates. Status complementarity is sometimes also expressed using gender symbolism, the Afa'afa'w being "male" as distinct from the "female" Ondondof. Clans belong to one ward moiety or the other.

The effect of the generic names is that the ward moieties crosscut the village-moiety division; all males are either Afa'afa'w or Ondondof, and each ward contains both moieties. Furthermore, the ward-moiety division introduces another refinement into the village-moiety opposition. For instance, Ililip and Balanga are ritual "enemies" to each other; but, it is the Ililip Afa'afa'w who in fact compete with the Balanga Afa'afa'w, and the Ililip Ondondof who compete with the Balanga Ondondof. Opposite ward moieties of "enemy" wards (e.g. Balanga Afa'afa'w and Ililip Ondondof) maintain an ambivalent "friendship" similar to that between wards of different moieties which are not directly opposed. The ward-moiety "friend" relationship thus mitigates the gross opposition between "enemy" wards at the village level. In the next chapter, I will illustrate how this mitigation operates in conventional competition.

Ward moieties also divide each ward into two geographically distinct halves. Afa'afa'w clans cluster in hamlets close to the central hub of the village, while Ondondof clans reside farther out on the "spokes." The two submoieties converge territorially near the geographical center of the ward (Figure 2). Here is located the major ceremonial hamlet, often on a site slightly elevated above adjacent hamlets and containing a spirit house of one of the five Tambaran grades. Unlike the other hamlets, this ceremonial precinct belongs to all the clans of the ward. It is the scene of formal and informal meetings, ceremonial yam displays and exchanges, and various Tambaran activities. When these latter activities are secretive, non-members must avoid the ceremonial hamlet and use by-passes winding around and below it. For this reason men usually avoid building dwelling houses in the ceremonial hamlet, even though they may have the right to do so.

The ward moieties' most important ritual work is pig hunting. Wild pork is essential in virtually all Tambaran ceremonies; and the supremely important task of catching wild pigs depends, it is thought, on powerful magic. Each moiety possesses pig magic, handed down patrilineally within one of the initiation partnerships (see below). The pig magician is keeper of the heavy nets associated with his magic. Each ward moiety owns a hunting reserve, a stretch of old forest roamed by the pigs associated with the magic. As mentioned in Chapter 2, these beasts are believed to have a child-like, sentimental attachment to the men of their ward moiety, especially the

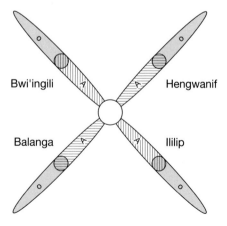

Figure 2 Schematic of Ilahita ward moieties

magician himself. It is said that the pigs in the reserve are attracted only by the magic of "their" moiety, implying that poaching with nets in another moiety's reserve would be a futile endeavor. Reflecting their residential orientation, Afa'afa'w reserves lie in areas near the village and Ondondof reserves are more distant.

The ward moieties of Ilahita, together with their constituent clans and membership numbers, are shown in Table 4; the heavy horizontal line designates the village-moiety division. Recalling Nangup's relatively recent arrival in the village (Chapter 5), note that the village-moiety division is internal to this ward, coinciding with the ward-moiety opposition; this was the device for adding the new ward to the village's dual organization, without disrupting the latter's symmetry. Specific ward-moiety names are not shown in Table 4. Suffice it to say that some of them are derived from the names of member clans, others from the names of member

Table 4 Ilahita ward moieties, showing constituent clans*

	Afa'afa'w	No.	Ondondof	No.
BALANGA	Laongol		Owapwi	
	Sahopwi	50	Bundahimbil	42
HENGWANIF	Owapwi		Sahopwi	
	Hengwanif	24	Afinga	29
NANGUP	Laongol			
	Tatemba			
	Bundahimbil	32		
NANGUP			Balangapwi	
			Eleputa	
			Indibi	27
ILILIP	Balangapwi		Balangapwi	
	Eleputa		Mano'um	
	Atefin		Sao'um	
	Indibi		Afenim	63
	Tata	71		
BWI'INGILI	Eleputa		Balangapwi	
	Tata	28	Indibi	26
TOTAL		205		187

* Names appearing more than once in the table refer to different clans having the same name

hamlets. In the case of Bwi'ingili, the ward moieties Kwalelimelipwi and Ambonipwi are named after two types of secret flutes, Ambon and Kwalelimel, which are in turn named after two bird species known for their distinctive cries: *ambon*, a red parrot, and *kwalelimel*, a kind of thrush. These names, and of course the clan-based names, impart a totemic aura to the ward moieties, which, as in the case of the village moieties, hints at the possibility that these categories are logically or historically derived from descent groups.

Initiation moieties

Just as the ward moieties cut across the village moieties, so the initiation moieties divide the village into two parts, called Sahopwas and Owapwas. The names signify "elder brothers" and "younger brothers," respectively. At the local level, this opposition occurs between the two subclans of a given clan: Sahopwasinguf ("line of the elder brothers") and Owapwasinguf ("line of the younger brothers"). Similarly, the Sahopwas–Owapwas dichotomy evokes the hierarchical relationship between brothers, whereby the elder exercises moral and legal authority over the younger. The senior group (Sahopwas) is defined as being the initiation moiety currently in possession of the penultimate grade of the Tambaran, Nggwal Bunafunei. These men will initiate their Owapwas partners into that grade, surrendering it to them at the next induction ceremony. At that time the names switch between the groups, as do their statuses and associated ritual roles. Thus, at one stage in the initiation cycle the Sahopwasinguf subclan may have Sahopwas ritual status; following the next Nggwal Bunafunei initiation, the Sahopwasinguf subclan becomes that of the ritually subordinate Owapwas moiety.

The initiation-moiety opposition is expressed through a multitude of hereditary initiation partnerships, operating between individuals or patrilines of complementary subclans. Thus, Ego is initiated by his father's partner in the opposite initiation moiety; later, Ego initiates this man's son; and, still later, this man's son initiates Ego's son. And so on. The resulting pattern of relationships can be seen in Figure 3. Note that, at any given ceremony, all of the hundreds of partnerships in the village are involved in this initiation-moiety transaction; Figure 3 shows only one of them.

Figure 3 shows the Tambaran cycle at an instant when, between the paired patrilines A and B, A_2 is the Sahopwas initiator and B_2 is the Owapwas junior partner, as yet naive to the Nggwal Bunafunei grade of the cult. Also shown is the father of A_2, who, if he is alive at all, is probably quite ancient. The man who initiated A_1 is most assuredly dead, as shown for B_0.

Sahopwas (A)   Owapwas (B)

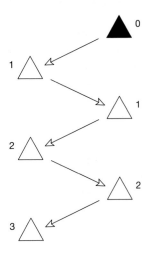

Figure 3 Initiation moieties

On the Figure, A_2 belongs to the cult grade currently in control of Nggwal Bunafunei. The son of A_2 is only just entering the lower grades, an entire cycle away from initiation into Nggwal Bunafunei. The father of B_2 is of the same moiety (Owapwas) as his son, but with the difference that he has seen Nggwal Bunafunei and was the one who showed it to A_2. These "senior" Owapwas are, in practice, the group in which supreme ritual authority resides, by virtue of possessing Nggwal Walipeine, the highest and most senior Tambaran grade. Their prerogative is also based on esoteric knowledge concerning the grade which A_2 formally controls. That is, although A_2 has seen Nggwal Bunafunei, he was not involved in the elaborate secret preparations for his own initiation. This includes the magical and technological aspects of erecting the spirit house, and also the skills of making carvings, paintings, and other paraphernalia. Person A_2 knows the secrets but does not yet fully understand them; neither is he capable of showing them to anyone else. The Sahopwas group (A_2) therefore continues to depend on their initiators (B_1) to show them how to perform the initiation on behalf of B_2. The men of B_1 will cease to be essential when A3 is due for initiation, at which time the names will have switched and A_2 will be acting as the senior Owapwas adviser; by then, most of the B_1 will be dead or very old. The formal structure of the initiation moieties, while founded on the dualistic opposition Sahopwas/Owapwas, thus embodies a three-part series: B_1, A_2, and B_2.[10]

Plate 27 Tambaran statuary is commissioned by subclans for presentation to their partner subclans at the latter's initiation into the Nggwal Bunafunei grade. Scores of these statues are carved by master artists for a single initiation ceremony.

Dualism and descent

I said earlier that initiation partnerships (Sahopwas–Owapwas) occur between dualistically paired subclans, Sahopwasinguf and Owapwasinguf. At this level the dual organization becomes enmeshed with the descent system of clans and subclans, even down to intrafamilial structures of sibling hierarchy. On the other hand, considering that village moieties have totems and that both they and the ward moieties are made up of clan clusters, one might regard the dual organization as a descent system in its entirety. Consider, also, that the spirits venerated in the Tambaran cult, while ostensibly of a distinct category, are ancestor-like in certain important respects, and that similar cult spirits among the neighboring Abelam are explicitly ancestral. More graphically, at the climactic moment of induction into Nggwal Bunafunei, initiates are brought into the secret interior of the spirit house, where they see, among other things, a massive display of paintings, mounted so as to comprise a wall hiding the supremely sacred inner sanctum of the house. Each painting represents a cult spirit, usually rendered in more or less human form; there is one painting for each adult male. By arranging the paintings in genealogical order, the gallery amounts to a gigantic descent chart of all adult males in the village!

Plate 28 In the Nggwal Bunafunei spirit house the inner sanctum is hidden behind a wall composed of hundreds of paintings, each belonging to a member of the grade. Arranged by degrees of genealogical proximity, the gallery amounts to a gigantic descent chart of the men of the village. The inner sanctum is the home of the pipes and drums shown in Photograph 6.

My sense is that Tambaran ideology is shot-through with descent overtones that are only dimly perceived, probably because the Ilahita failed to grasp the ancestral nature of Tambaran spirits when they imported the institution from the Abelam back in the nineteenth century; other elements underwent similar "mistranslations" (Tuzin 1995). Rather than faithfully adopting Abelam ideology, the Ilahita made the Tambaran into something separate, something superior to everything else. In doing so, they may have stumbled on a new and more powerfully integrative ritual construction: a cult whose spirits patronized not only the individual clans but, in aggregate, the entire village as a spiritual unity. The cult's infrastructure, the dual organization, is simultaneously a ritual formation and a descent formation. By idiomatically connecting the Tambaran with the timeless, everyday things of kinship and descent, the dual organization wove a system of cultural meaning of remarkable strength, resilience, and operational effectiveness.

Lower-level dual structures

It must be emphasized that all cult initiations involve immense flows of feast foods – primarily yams and pork – between initiation partners. From the start of the initiation observances, which may last for weeks, it is the senior partners who must "feed" their junior charges; at the conclusion of the initiation, the latter reciprocate by sponsoring comparable feasts for their initiators, in gratitude for the ritual work they had done earlier.

At the risk of complicating an already complicated structure, I must mention a second type of exchange partnership which is apparently independent of the initiation system and operates solely in food exchanges. In addition to an initiation partner most men have one or more secondary exchange partners. Men linked in this relationship should belong to the same ward moiety, though they need not be fellow clansmen. Food exchanges primarily occur between initiation partners, but a smaller quantity of yams is simultaneously presented to one's secondary partner. If a man gives a larger share of yams to his secondary partner, his initiation partner is entitled to rebuke him for being disrespectful. Another point is that the secondary partnership is not bound by inheritance: men may form such a relationship, but their sons are not obliged to carry it forward, and may instead select secondary partners of their choice.

Dualism and demography

An intriguing possibility is that the secondary partnership marks the tentative beginning of yet another level of dual organization; perhaps the others started in this way, as well. For it is highly significant to the evolutionary line of my argument that the secondary-partnership system operates only in the two largest wards, Balanga and Ililip. When asked why they did not also have secondary partnerships, one Hengwanif man replied, "Look around. How many men do you see in Hengwanif? We are very few and have trouble even supporting our initiation partners. Ililip and Balanga have secondary partnerships but we are too small."

Here we have it: explicit confirmation that the dual organization is, at its structural roots, closely responsive to population sizes, and that, as such, the integrating effects of its many ritual and competitive functions have fundamentally contributed to the growth and maintenance of the village. Just as the organization in Hengwanif and Bwi'ingili is a shade simpler than in Balanga and Ililip, because the manpower of those wards cannot support a more complicated system, so the other Ilahita Arapesh villages are organized to levels of complexity commensurate with their population sizes. For example, other villages have only two wards, and are without the separate structures I am calling "ward moieties"; ritual functions assigned to Ilahita ward moieties are, in other places, carried out by village or initiation moieties. Likewise, having only two named wards, other villages lack the "enemy"/"friend" refinements that crosscut the Ilahita village-moiety divide.

Ilahita's larger population also enables it to support a Tambaran grade that no other village has: Nggwal Walipeine, the Tambaran of old men. With this innovation, Ilahita created a class of ritually supreme elders, men who in other places have advanced out the top of the initiation series, are retired from ritual affairs, and are virtually powerless.[11] In Ilahita, however, there are enough men in this age cohort (approximately 45 years and older) to execute the architectural, artistic, ritual, and feasting works necessary to support a separate, viable Tambaran grade. Contrary to my expectation before going to the village, Ilahita's evolutionary success did not entail a centralization of secular political authority in the form of chiefs or super-big men, but it did produce a centralization of ritual authority in the form of this class of cult elders. One secular consequence of this development – intentional or not – was to equip Ilahita with a ritual structure of social control that contributed mightily to village solidarity. We now turn to this and other instances of the dual organization and its patron, the Tambaran, in actual operation.

Plate 29 In the Nggwal Walipeine spirit house, the inner sanctum is a free-standing enclosure located in the center of the floor.

Plate 30 Detail of structure in Plate 29. The leafy forms represent aquatic plants, symbolizing (1) the watery medium in which the ancestral dead supposedly reside, and (2) the taro leaf that was used to conceal the decrepit First Man in the story of Nambweapa'w. The predominantly white coloration also signifies old age: the ashy white skin proverbially acquired by elder people from sleeping near the hearth. Nggwal Walipeine is the tambaran of old men.

7 The ritual road to hierarchy

The ritual dimension of social life

Social institutions, such as academia or politics, are analytical concepts – abstractions, useful sociological constructs that refer to sectors in which major activities in a society are organized. One drawback to always thinking about society in institutional terms, however, is the tendency to *reify* institutions, that is, to attribute to these analytical concepts a concreteness – a "thingness" – they do not possess in observable behavior. For example, although Wall Street journalists and professional economists may define a field of study as "economics" or talk about "the economy," referring to phenomena they consider to be of great importance, few are zealous enough to believe that any action can be purely economic. They know that other, non-economic considerations are always involved. Thus, power relations, social class, and aesthetic values may also influence individual choices affecting, at a collective level, the formation of wealth and the movement of goods and services. Similarly, political action in the real world is rarely devoid of other factors, such as wealth differentials, ethnic or regional identities, religious values, and even kinship loyalties. In the light of the inherent fuzziness of institutional boundaries, it behooves us to regard "economic," "political," and other such concepts less as *categories* of social action, and more as *dimensions* of potentially any and all social action.

These thoughts apply with particular force to small-scale societies such as Ilahita, where many relationships bear multiple dimensions. In technical language, such relationships are termed *multiplex*.[1] Consider the case of religion, which in Ilahita is especially prominent. In our own relatively secular society, religion for most people is something which, at most, concerns them on the Sabbath, on certain holidays, and in ritual observances surrounding events such as weddings and funerals. Likewise, the Tambaran is at the fore during the months- or years-long ritual seasons of initiation, when ceremonial practices involving ritual and cosmological understandings dominate virtually all other concerns. But the influence of the Tambaran also overflows its sabbath and pervades nearly all of social life and ideology. The sheer fact that cult orthodoxy rigidly excludes women from sacred contexts, thus defining them as separate from – by implication inferior to – men and supernaturals, is reason enough to expect that ritual understandings strongly influence everyday life.

To a remarkable extent, however, the anti-feminine violence of Tambaran rhetoric is not matched at the domestic level, where actual relations between husbands and wives, fathers and (uninitiated) children are nurturant, respectful, and often affectionate. These positive sentiments appear to be very old in the culture. In the aftermath of the destruction of the Tambaran in 1984, it became plain that cult ideology had actually fostered domestic tranquility, both by sheltering the fragility of masculine egos behind a wall of cult secrecy, and by providing an outlet for otherwise destructive male aggression.[2] For without those protections and sublimations, masculine aggression had nowhere to go but home, which is why the incidences of wife- and mother-beating rose sharply after the Tambaran cult had been abolished (Tuzin 1997).

While the Tambaran's influence over the intimacies of family life was surprisingly slight, its penetration of other areas of social life and ideology was not slight at all; in fact, it was virtually complete. When I first lived in Ilahita (1969–72), men did not grow yams and hunt pigs simply for nourishment, but as food for the Tambaran in the great secluded feasts the men hosted and in which they shared. For that matter, men did not catch or produce food only to consume it, but to present it to one of several hereditary exchange partners, according to a structure of reciprocity dictated, as we have seen, by the Tambaran. And what did these ritual exchange feasts accomplish, other than the full bellies of men and of spirits? Nothing less, said the Arapesh, than the Tambaran's renewal of all species' fertility, and rebestowal of material prosperity, happiness, and spiritual vitality on the village. Men did not organize themselves into totemic clans, subclans, moieties, submoieties, partnerships, wards, and villages merely by accident or for the sake of social convenience, but because each of these units had a designated role in the ritual work of the Tambaran. Boys did not naturally grow into men, and men into old men: masculinity was acquired, fulfilled, and retired through a series of five Tambaran initiations, carrying the male from his mother's arms to the gates of great old age (Tuzin 1980, 1982).

The Tambaran also ruled over matters of blood and argument. Wars were fought for various mundane ends, but always under the aegis of the Tambaran. The magical power conjured by war sorcerers was that of the Tambaran, not themselves; killings in battles and raids were credited to the Tambaran, not to the human victor, who remained anonymous; trophies of enemy body parts were mounted on the Tambaran's house, or around the neck of someone costumed as a Tambaran spirit, not on a warrior's belt (Harrison 1993: 85). It would not be going too far to say that the Tambaran was a cult of war and human sacrifice; the Tambaran's ability to bestow fertility and prosperity depended on the occasional "eating" of enemy dead.[3] Equally, though, it was a cult of peace: only the Tambaran was authorized to proclaim truces between enemy villages, usually to allow hostile groups to cooperate in initiations and other major ceremonial endeavors.[4]

Disputes within the village, especially when they set groups against one another, also caught the attention of the Tambaran. Resolution was attained by "summoning the Tambaran" (i.e. mounting a convocation of cult members) to preside over the speaking, singing, and feasting duels that would decide who won and who paid a fine. In other cases the Tambaran might be summoned to punish an individual for violating sumptuary or behavioral rules laid down by the cult: sporting a netbag design that belonged to another ritual group; wearing a red hibiscus rather than the yellow variety to which one is ritually entitled; recklessly using a thatch weave on one's house that was of a technique or design used on the spirit house of a grade other than one's own; planting a long yam using excavation techniques that were the property of a Tambaran grade senior to one's own – these and numerous other offenses, because they disturbed the ritual order, were punishable by payments of feast foods to the group whose rights were trespassed upon.

Do not suppose that these were rare occurrences. As in our own society, where the proliferation of laws *increases* the amount and range of litigation, in Ilahita the ways of transgressing against Tambaran doctrine were legion; so much so that it was nearly impossible to avoid violating some rule or other from time to time. Furthermore, being unwritten and very subject to interpretation by competing interests, the "rules" themselves were Kafkaesque in their indeterminacy. Rather than the promulgator of a rigid law code to which people dutifully submitted – or else – the Tambaran presided over a rather squishy body of procedural understandings through which litigation could be framed, conducted, and brought to reasonably satisfactory conclusion. In the end, it all depended on the willingness of the "losing side" to submit to the broader consensus, as articulated by the cult elders, and not carry forward their grudge.

As an agent of social control the Tambaran also exploited naturally occurring events to further its ends. For example, when a death occurred in the village, sorcery was nearly always the presumed cause; but, as we will see presently, in many cases divination by cult elders revealed that the sorcerer had been acting as the Tambaran's appointed executioner, administering punishment for some remembered violation of ritual values or cult protocol. In the process, the vigilance and jealous powers of the Tambaran and its priestly stewards – the elders of the cult – were reaffirmed, and people were duly warned that violations of cult doctrine would eventually be punished.

The problem of sorcery

We have seen how the Tambaran welds the units of Ilahita society into a cooperating, mechanical whole. As another example of its unifying practices, consider the case of sorcery, a domain in which Tambaran beliefs once functioned (see below) to stabilize and structure Ilahita society. Before illustrating these social-control effects with particular instances, let me emphasize that sorcery beliefs are extremely threatening to neighborhood peace, especially in places such as Ilahita, where it is assumed that the sorcerer is either someone close to the victim, or in league with someone close enough to secure and pass on personal leavings – nail or hair clippings, saliva, sexual fluids, something chewed upon, and the like. In Western society, death by natural causes and other misfortunes – disease, accident, and plain bad luck – are not blamed on the secret envy or hatred of one's neighbors. In Ilahita, as in most New Guinea societies, they are. Only the deaths of the very old or very young are ascribed to "natural" causes, or, more likely, to no cause at all; all others, whatever the apparent cause, are assumed to be the result of foul play.

Under these paranoiac circumstances, one can easily imagine how a death or other serious misfortune could plunge the community into fear and disruptive suspicion. The identity of the sorcerer is sought by divinatory means.[5] When that identity is revealed, accusations and counterattacks frequently ensue, causing the social situation to deteriorate even further.[6] In the oral history of settlement changes in other villages in the vicinity, sorcery accusations are by far the most common cause cited for the dissolution of residential communities. Ilahita appears to have largely escaped this fate, thanks to the appreciation of generations of leaders that security lay in unity and numbers, and that external enemies would surely descend upon any segments that detached themselves from the main village. Sorcery was an ever-present worry, but the alternative was seen to be worse.

The cessation of warfare in the early 1950s tamed this hostile environment and created a situation in which sorcery-related disputes could play havoc with village unity. And yet, this did not happen: although the decades of the 1950s and 1960s witnessed some dismantling of the village's nucleated structure, individuals who removed themselves to bush camps in the hinterland rarely did so in response to sorcery entanglements. Sorcery beliefs continued unabated, but their socially deleterious effects were now moderated in a new and different way. For it was during the first decade of pacification that Nggwal, his supply of enemy dead no longer forthcoming, began symbolically to feast on his own people.

This gruesome turn of events was nonetheless highly adaptive for village solidarity. The reason is that the invocation of Tambaran ethics on the occasion of death converts a supposedly man-made calamity into one governed by superhuman agencies. What was seen as an act of hatred or wickedness is recast as an act consistent with the divined motives of the Tambaran, as a kind of ritual execution. In its effects, the response resembles a naturalistic explanation for death: the mood of the crisis shifts from revenge to resignation on the part of the aggrieved; revenge against the suspected sorcerer is declared illegal and irrelevant; and the potential for community dissolution is removed. Consider, then, the following cases.

Cases: death and the Tambaran

Case 1

Leitipen, a woman of about 50, was the wife of an important man and the mother of five sons, three of whom were married at the time of her death. Approximately a month before Leitipen died, two of her daughters-in-law fell ill with identical symptoms, an understandable coincidence since the women were constantly in each other's company. As the younger women started to recover, Leitipen began displaying the same symptoms. Within a fortnight they were well, and she was dead.

On the evening of her burial one of the neighborhood diviners went into a trance in which he was supposedly possessed by the spirit of his dead grandfather. During the trance, he sang the song of a Nggwal spirit of Leitipen's husband's clan. Afterward a number of cult elders belonging to various clans met to ponder the meaning of the song's occurrence during the trance. Their eventual interpretation was accepted by everyone, including, most importantly, the dead woman's primary avengers, her bereaved husband and sons.

Three years before, it was recalled, a Tambaran feast had been held in the village. Such events may continue intermittently for weeks, and the women's task is to prepare soup and other foods which, they are told, the men will feed to Nggwal. Leitipen's sons commanded their wives to make soup "for Nggwal." The women angrily replied that they were weary of working so hard for Nggwal, and if Nggwal was hungry he could eat feces. This was a serious blasphemy, much publicized, and the women were soundly beaten by their husbands.

In the opinion of the investigating cult elders, Leitipen's death was a delayed Tambaran retribution for this offense. The daughters-in-law were being punished and surely would have died, had not Leitipen by some mysterious altruistic means drawn the sickness to herself. Leitipen was fondly hailed as a great and good woman, but there was no attempt to avenge her death.

Case 2

Songwanda'a was a youth of 16 when he died of what appeared (to me) to be cerebral malaria. He left his middle-aged parents, a younger brother, and two older married sisters. The divination procedure involved viewing Songwanda'a's dead body some hours after it had been placed in an open grave. When this was done it was noticed that pale gray markings on the corpse's skin resembled the body designs used during Nggwal ceremonies.[7]

Some years earlier, it was recalled, preparations had been under way for a Nggwal ceremony in the hamlet of Songwanda'a's father, Gaiapo. Just before the festivities were to begin, Gaiapo got into a fearful row with his wife, Kowala. In the heated exchange, Kowala was heard to say, "You are an old man, weak and with white hair. How can you hope to satisfy me [sexually]?" The insult against her husband's virility was made sacrilegious by the imminence of Nggwal. Kowala's final punishment was the loss of her son.

A sorcery bundle, said to have been found concealed nearby in the forest, was produced at the deathbed. With this evidence, Gaiapo had the option of performing retaliatory sorcery through the agency of the dead boy's ghost. Having learned, however, that Nggwal was implicated in the affair, he abandoned whatever plans he may have had for revenge. Vague rumors circulated that the husband of one of Songwanda'a's sisters had performed the sorcery, but these evaporated without, apparently, affecting Gaiapo's relationship with that son-in-law. The sorcery bundle and the identity of the sorcerer no longer mattered.

Case 3

Ku'umbwili and Imul were initiation partners, both clients of the Nggwal spirit Nimbea. They died within a week of one another, which alone suggested that their deaths were linked. The grave inspection and trance divination left no doubt of it. Indeed, the hideous sore in Imul's throat which caused him to die of starvation lent itself to the community interpretation of their deaths. Their joint offense was to have confounded the strict separation between the initiation moieties.

A decade previous to their deaths, Imul had brought Ku'umbwili to a Tambaran ceremony which he was ineligible to attend. Because such a deed cannot be undone, Ku'umbwili became in effect identical in ritual rank to Imul. There was much public consternation over this, because the action potentially disrupted the orderly succession of their descendants. At the time, Imul had no explanation for his mistake. Years later, his death signified that it was his voice, in telling Ku'umbwili to come to the forbidden ceremony, that had, in a manner of speaking, removed their partnership from this world to the next.

More cases could be cited (see Tuzin 1980: 290–3). In each instance, the complicity of Tambaran spirits – revealed by oracular means controlled by cult elders – indicated that the deceased or someone close to him or her had committed some act offensive to the Tambaran and punishable by death. Aggrieved kinsmen were denied redress under sanctions of public disapproval and Tambaran vengeance. Thus death, which in a climate heavy with sorcery beliefs might have led to severe community unrest, was forestalled in its effects by the action of a countervailing set of beliefs. Capitalizing on the mystery and implied violence of death, the Tambaran made the sorcerer its henchman and firmly established itself in an area of experience which, before the cessation of warfare and human sacrifice, had been outside its sphere of interest. Sorcery remained the immediate cause of death, but it was now referred to a more ultimate Cause: the Tambaran. Natural death was effectively retrieved from human will and was made a sign of supernatural disapproval and punishment. Thus, the ideology operated both to confirm the efficacy of sorcery and to blunt its social and psychological effects, while at the same time strengthening the authority of the elders.

From the standpoint of social evolution, this expansion of Tambaran consciousness significantly featured the emergence of a *rationalized religious ethic* – a body of doctrine against which behavior could be compared, evaluated, and, if necessary, punished; a body of doctrine, moreover, which summarized and transcended the level of individual clan spirits. In other words, from out of the many individual and competing clan tambarans, there emerged a capitalized Tambaran, a transcendent spirit that patronized the entire village and allied itself with the elders of the cult, the men of Nggwal Walipeine. To my knowledge, both this theological innovation and its associated cult grade of elderhood are unique to Ilahita; and it is clear that their operations have importantly contributed to the social integrity of this large village.

Ritually prescribed harmony

The relentless work of the Tambaran is to promote its own power and relevance, the special knowledge and authority of cult elders, the ritual order of ranked statuses based on sex, age, and initiatory standing, and, most important, peace and tranquility in the village. This last point was graphically illustrated during the construction of a massive Nggwal Bunafunei spirit house that I once witnessed. A climactic moment in such a project is the hoisting of a hardwood ridgepole, weighing hundreds of kilograms, into nearly horizontal position about 15 meters above ground. The technique consists of lashing betelnut trunks to the tops of a line of upright breadfruit trunks that serve as a temporary scaffolding down the center of what will be the house floor. Sturdy lawyer vines are carried up and over the betelnut fulcrum, and their ends are attached to the hardwood ridgepole. Teams of men on the ground grasp each vine and, in a coordinated fashion, hoist the ridgepole up to the level of the betelnut trunk, assisted by other men pushing up with heavy sticks or lifting with their shoulders as they climb and perch up the breadfruit poles.

On this particular occasion, the ridgepole had been hoisted about halfway up, when the lawyer vines began snapping – an alarming event, both for the danger it posed to workers below and for the implication that cult spirits were withholding support for, or even sabotaging, the project. The ridgepole was stabilized and hastily lashed in place, halfway up the poles, and the men gathered in the clearing to discuss what might be causing the problem.

Immediately, it was decided that someone must be nursing a grudge against someone else or harboring ill will against the construction project itself. A few of the cult elders took charge and carefully asked each man, publicly and in turn, whether he had any negative feelings. Each man professed to feeling nothing but sincere solidarity with the project and his fellow-workers. Perhaps, thought the elders, the man in question is hiding his negative feelings, or is unaware that he has them. It was decided that an impromptu pig feast would solve the problem by surely making everyone feel good. A collection was raised to sponsor a pig feast right then and there. Later that day, when the men, fat and happy, returned to their comradely labors, the ridgepole was hoisted the rest of the way quickly and without further mishap.

Plate 31 After discussing and meditating on an accident that occurred during spirit-house construction, the master artists, who are also masters of ritual protocol, slap the ground to seal their collective magic of deliverance.

This case exemplifies an axiom of Tambaran ideology, namely, that the magical effectiveness of all ritual – whether raising a ridgepole or renewing the fertility of all species – crucially requires harmony among the participants. For a community of men that is, and describes itself as being, chronically fractious and competitive, the mounting of successful, large-scale collective projects, such as spirit-house constructions, major ceremonies, and war, is nothing short of miraculous. No wonder the men experience these achievements with a sense of spiritual renewal and empowerment. I once asked an old warrior why Ilahita had always defeated its enemies in battle. Instead of appealing to superior numbers or fighting ability, as I would have expected, the man made a sweeping gesture at the spirit house that towered next to where we stood. "See," he said, "it is because of the power of the spirits that we won battles. The house is proof that the spirits are with us!" Allowing for the religious idiom, he was right.

Exhilarating as these moments of spiritual accord are, the men know that their effects will not last. Once the house is built, or the ceremony completed, or the battle won, life returns to its normal pace. Petty squabbles break out, factionalism re-emerges, new trespasses and resentments begin to accumulate (Rappaport 1968: 116). In ritual idiom, the men imagine this social decline to be caused by the progressive weakening

Plate 32 The huge task of coordinating the construction of a spirit house lays the organizational groundwork for other collective enterprises, such as ceremonial performances, exchange, and war.

of the Tambaran, its skin and muscle slackening as it becomes hungrier and hungrier since the last feeding. Eventually, the parallel processes of the social deterioration of the community and the "bodily" deterioration of the Tambaran reach a point where the men decide that corrective action is needed: a Tambaran event involving major collective works and massive feasting. Most vociferous in calling for the Tambaran are men who provided ritual services last time and who are owed a return of equivalent services by their exchange partners. Thus, although the pattern of cult activities is based on a structured cycling of reciprocal obligations, the actual rhythm is decided not so much by *that* structure, as by the informal, but highly reliable, dynamics of discontent and divisiveness inherent in village social life. Obversely, the fact that these ritual remedies are actually curative and restorative of the body social verifies the importance of the Tambaran to the integrity of Ilahita village. Later, we will encounter another example of actions in one arena supporting structures in another.

This chapter has thus far dealt with the Tambaran in its ritual guise: the direct effects of religious ideas on social life; in particular, their invocation at times of crisis, maintenance of village solidarity, and self-serving interpretation by cult elders jealous of their authority. The work of the

Tambaran does not stop at the ritual boundary, however. The dual organization, while primarily defined as the framework for ritual categories and activities, carries Tambaran charisma into the otherwise secular arenas of everyday competition and aggression, channeling them in ways that actually promote the good of the village. Moreover, the application of ritual structures to mundane affairs reminds people of the validity of the Tambaran, even when the context is not strictly religious or cosmological. Before illustrating these workings, a further structural feature of the dual organization must be considered, namely, its symmetry.

The dual organization in balance

The secondary exchange partnerships mentioned at the end of the previous chapter disclosed the practical importance of numerical balance in the dual organization considered *as a system*. The various crosscutting structures may be viewed as a village-wide grid that is divided into ever finer levels of social discrimination. The minimal "cells," the irreducible units, are the groups of male siblings, or occasionally single individuals.[8] At any one time a number of the cells may, for various reasons, be empty: a man may die without sons, leaving his partners without partners; a man may go off to the plantation and not come back; a clan may become extinct, thus removing an entire subset of cells. The continuation of the system as a whole depends on keeping the number of empty cells to a minimum. This is what the Hengwanif man in Chapter 6 was saying: if Hengwanif were to institute secondary partnerships, they would not survive because that ward has insufficient personnel to support them; too many of the cells would be chronically empty. Exchange obligations would go unmet, and eventually that particular exchange structure would be abolished as unworkable.

Because each of its eight layers features the exchange of ritual goods and services, the dual organization operates most smoothly when the reciprocating units are approximately equal in size. But because these are essentially descent units, with membership determined by birth, the system is prey to demographic imbalances. Nature cannot be relied upon to give everyone an equal number of sons. Accordingly, the system of structural oppositions must contain mechanisms to correct numerical imbalances and, when necessary, replenish empty cells in the grid. Demographic strains are first felt at the finer structural levels, particularly in the initiation partnerships, where adjustments must follow immediately upon the parties' perceiving incipient imbalances. More than that, a wise and responsible man anticipates years ahead that events in his own or the next generation will upset the initiation partnership, and he takes steps to forestall serious difficulties. The untimely death of a young man, the lack of male heirs of another, the disruptive Christian conversion of a third – these are stresses which beset the system, in response to which structural flexibility is essential.

That the system adjusts itself in response to demographic imbalances is indicated by the figures in Table 5, which shows the membership totals of initiation moieties and submoieties (the "Junior"/"Senior" opposition within the initiation moiety). At first glance the system appears to be on the verge of major disequilibrium, coming at the next turn in the cycle. Thus, the Sahopwas Juniors will become Owapwas Seniors and, as such, greatly outnumber (175 to 95) the men who will have become the new Sahopwas Juniors. In practice this does not happen: many of the Sahopwas Juniors are already elderly men and will not live to assume the status of Owapwas Senior. Indeed, it is likely that death will cut their numbers in half by the time of the next turn in the cycle, thus maintaining the balance.[9] The Sahopwas Senior category is correspondingly occupied by very old men who first saw Nggwal at quite a young age.

Table 5 Ilahita initiation moieties and submoieties, showing membership totals

SAHOPWAS (Total = 193)		OWAPWAS (Total = 189)	
Junior	Senior	Junior	Senior
175	18	95	94

The difference between the totals for the Sahopwas and Owapwas groups being so slight (1.04 percent), there seems good reason to suspect that the groups have been manipulated in the interests of numerical symmetry. That is, some people were apparently moved to different groups, with the result that symmetrically paired groups remain more or less symmetrical in size, as well. This seems to occur at the most local level, especially. Thus, ward moieties as localized in the wards are more symmetrical than village moieties which are localized in the village; and the initiation moieties, localized in the clans, possess nearly perfect symmetry.[10] This is because imbalances at the finer levels are more conspicuous to men engaged in the ritual partnerships and, as will be seen in the next section, more accessible to corrective manipulation. Because the three dual levels are vertically interrelated, symmetry at the finest level of initiation partnerships contributes to symmetry at levels of greater structural inclusiveness.

Underlying this view is the assumption that structural and numerical symmetry is a conscious goal in the workings of the dual organization. In a previous chapter we saw that the principle of symmetry was applied to the incorporation of Nangup ward into the dual organization of the main village. But such high-level, large-scale alignments are too rare and too potentially disruptive to be effective in keeping the system routinely in balance. Rather, it is by constantly tweaking the lowest-level, finest gears that considerations of symmetry – or, perhaps more accurately, *conscious considerations of reciprocity* – keep the entire system humming along.

With this notion of "system maintenance" in mind, let us turn to the subject of adoption, which is a very widespread practice in Ilahita.[11] There are several lines of relevance connecting adoption with the dual organization. First, adoption is an important mechanism in maintaining the numerical balances upon which the dual organization depends. Second, adoption confirms that the dual organization deals not only with large structures such as village moieties, but also reaches down to the grassroots of village society, into decisions taken within families, thus vertically integrating the community from bottom to top. Third, adoption highlights the interface between the dual organization and marriage exchange – echoes of a former time, perhaps, when initiation (i.e. intraclan) moieties were exogamous and the system of marriage was prescriptive (Chapter 6). In present practice, the shuffling of boys and girls between families has the dual effect of providing marriage-exchange partners for everyone *and* providing men with initiation partners. Finally, adoption, especially as seen in the case to be presented, frequently serves the incidental, but highly beneficial, purpose of placing predictably ambitious, rivalrous brothers – the sons of great men – into opposed ritual classes. By this mechanism, anti-social aggression is channeled into ritually productive pathways, and the dual organization deals with an important vulnerability in Ilahita and any other kinship-based society, namely, the behavioral risks surrounding sibling solidarity.

Before proceeding, let me explain that adoption in Ilahita society is a purely legal event, with little effect on the adoptee's experiences in growing up. If a male is adopted by his father's brother – a common occurrence – this simply means that he is marked to inherit that man's lands and groves, rather than those of his biological father. Upon entering adolescence, he will begin to work with that man, who will familiarize him with the lands, groves, and magic spells that will one day be his. Not only is a change of residence unnecessary; chances are, because brothers tend to live together, adoptee, biological father, and adoptive father would all live in the same hamlet, anyway.

Whereas sons are desirable as heirs and protectors, daughters are desirable as assistants in gardening and child-care, and also to provide creature comforts, such as water and firewood and cooked food, for elderly parents. The following example is fairly typical (Tuzin 1976: 95).

One man in early middle age, with four sons and no daughter, lovingly fondled the infant daughter of his wife's brother and announced, beaming, that an adoption had been agreed to, and that when the girl grew up she would be his daughter and look after him in his old age. I helpfully noted that when his four sons married he would have at least four daughters-in-law close at hand to do his bidding, but this he rejected imperiously. "What are daughters-in-law? Such women are mean and selfish, and desire your death. A *daughter* will care for you as no one else will!"

In some cases, adoption occurs to settle a marriage debt. A man without a sister to exchange for a wife might promise a child of the union as delayed compensation for her. If male, the child will take up residence with his mother's group upon reaching early adulthood. Given the high rate of village endogamy (93 percent), he is not likely to have to go far. If female, the child will not move at all, but will become available to her mother's group as a "sister" for their marriage-exchange purposes.

Adoption and system symmetry

A basic tenet of the initiation partnership is that a man and his brothers inherit the same partners and cooperate as a unit in respect of them. Does this rule apply without exception? Table 6 shows that, although the majority of fraternal pairs participate in the same initiation unit, a substantial minority (35 percent) do not.[12] This being the case, what justice is there in treating the fraternal group as the irreducible unit of ritual action? In a statistical sense, none. Nevertheless, the ideological statement that this is so is quite emphatic: when presented with the fact that many brothers are variously *opposed* to one another in the system, informants insist that these are aberrant cases. Necessity, it appears, has required that certain men change their ritual affiliations. What are the circumstances of such action, and how is the proper distribution of personnel maintained in the dual system?

Table 6 Ritual corporateness of fraternal siblings

Sibling dyads	Same group	Opposite group	Same/Opposite*
52	34 (65%)	15 (29%)	3 (6%)

* Refers to pairs in which brothers belong to the same initiation moiety, but are an entire cycle apart in initiation *sub*moiety standing. For example, one brother is an Owapwas Senior, the other an Owapwas Junior. Describing how this would come about would take us off the track of the study (but see Tuzin 1976)

A man without sons appoints male heirs for several reasons. The most obvious is as a way of distributing his material assets to men who will care for him in old age and propitiate him after death. If a man has daughters only, he benefits himself by trading one of them for another man's son (providing that the second man has sons to spare), thus giving each party an improved position in marriage exchange. Finally, were a man to die without male heirs, it would be a blow to his initiation partners, who depend upon the ritual relationship continuing on into future generations. It is in their interest and that of the Tambaran spirit they share that an heir be appointed.

Similarly, a man successful in sons – three or four who have survived toddlerhood – comes under pressure to offer one for adoption. The bargain is usually struck with an agnate comparably successful in daughters. If one of his own brothers is without any children at all, the man is expected to offer him a son without requiring anything in return. Moreover, if the person in need of an heir is the eldest brother in the sibling group, then the heir given to him should likewise be the eldest in his generation. The notion is that the heir to the eldest male in the present generation should be the eldest male in the next generation.

Adoption within the immediate agnatic group can result in a change of ritual affiliation for the adoptee if the boy's father and his adoptive father (i.e. father's brother) are in opposed initiation groups. As Table 6 has shown, it is not unusual for this situation to occur. This is what happened, for example, in the case of the brothers To'ongolal and Kunai.

Case: ritual implications of adoption

To'ongolal and Kunai are ambitious men, aged about 45 and 36, respectively. Both are polygynous, To'ongolal having two wives, Kunai six. Kunai's eldest son (by his senior wife), Atitapwin, is about 14 years old at the time of my census (Figure 4). Waipisi, their father, is an old man who, in his lifetime, had come to occupy a center position between the two initiation moieties. For prestige reasons, that is, he took over the initiation partnership of a deceased clansman and thereafter operated the exchange system in both directions at once. This requires much industry and many yams, and it is only the most successful and politically ambitious men who take on such a responsibility.[13]

A few years ago Waipisi converted to Christianity and withdrew from the ritual system. Following custom, his hereditary initiation partnership was bestowed upon his eldest son, To'ongolal; his acquired partnership was passed to Kunai. This action put the two brothers into opposite initiation moieties, and in fact To'ongolal was in the group that initiated Kunai into Nggwal Bunafunei. Kunai and To'ongolal were not, however, *direct* partners in the sharing and exchange of a particular Tambaran spirit (of the Nggwal grade) and its paraphernalia. For, when Waipisi assumed the prestigious middle position, he did so by acquiring another Nggwal spirit. This would, of course, have been the only feasible way of taking the middle position: if Waipisi had assumed both initiation statuses with respect to the same Nggwal spirit, he would have been exchanging with himself – and not even the exchanging of like for like ever goes that far! In other words, Waipisi's ritual loyalties were not contradictory, but operated in different directions. This is why his sons, though belonging to opposite moieties, were not pitted directly against one another in initiation ceremonies and exchange.

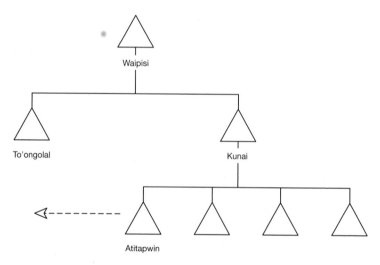

Figure 4 Atitapwin's adoption

Let me interrupt the case to make some points about Waipisi's taking of the middle position. First, it is through such prestige-seeking actions that the ritual alignments in the society become out of kilter with the clan structures. That is, each clan is identified with particular Nggwal spirits and sets of associated paraphernalia; ideally, therefore, men of different clans belong to different ritual "corporations." If, however, Waipisi assumes the middle position *vis-à-vis* his hereditary Nggwal and the Nggwal of *another* clan, his descendants will "segment" ritually while remaining members of the same (Waipisi's) clan. By the time of my study few enough men had taken the middle position that descent and ritual categories were still quite coterminous. One could imagine, however, that if the practice were to become more generalized, ritual identity could cease to have anything to do with membership in this or that clan. Such an evolutionary process must have occurred when the dual organization ceased to regulate marriage, that is, in the shift from prescriptive to proscriptive marriage practices (Chapter 6).

Another point to be made about Waipisi's action is that it placed his sons in opposite initiation moieties, thus alleviating behavioral tensions which appear frequently in the fraternal relationship. By requiring co-operation between brothers *vis-à-vis* their initiation partners, the ritual system grounds itself on the unreliable foundation of fraternal amity. Success of the ritual unit, and honor in the face of its partners, depend on the industry and good fortune of all members. If by laziness or bad luck one of the members is unable to contribute his share of yams to the exchange, or if he is incompetent in the manufacture of ritual paraphernalia, he is a burden both to his brothers and to his initiation partners. Such a man, it is said, will die from sorcery before he is very old. The element of scapegoating in the situation is much intensified if pre-existing tensions exist in the fraternal relationship.

By placing To'ongolal and Kunai in opposite initiation moieties, Waipisi incidentally (and probably unwittingly) reduced the potential for conflict between the brothers. As members of opposite groups, To'ongolal and Kunai are frequently able to act out their mutual antagonism – assuming such antagonism exists – in the ritualized aggression, competition, and defamation operating in the initiation-moiety relationship. The adaptation is particularly appropriate to To'ongolal and Kunai because, as the sons of a great man, they are highly ambitious themselves, prone to compete with one another with some fervor. The Ilahita themselves recognize that great men are frequently the sons of great men, with ambitions established early in life by inheriting the father's hot blood and subsequently following his example. A man who takes the middle position is by definition a great man, and the consequence of placing his sons in opposite classes has an ameliorative effect on their predictable behavior. Direct competition and hostility are thus redirected into a ritual field where such behavior is assigned positive value in the culture. With 29 percent of sibling pairs being divided in this way (Table 6), we may conclude that a significant amount of fraternal tension – latent or overt – is harmlessly released through the ritual system.

To continue with the Waipisi case:

> To'ongolal reached early middle age without any children. A daughter was given to him by a subclansman with daughters to spare; Kunai offered To'ongolal his first son, Atitapwin, as a male heir. This

entailed a ritual promotion for Atitapwin, in that he joined the Owapwas Junior submoiety one cycle down from his adoptive father. Accordingly, he would be initiated into the Nggwal grade a half-cycle before he would have been, had he remained Kunai's son. It also meant that Kunai would be in the group initiating Atitapwin and the submoiety into which he was promoted.[14]

As a result of these adoptions To'ongolal received a son and a daughter who would care for him in old age, and who could use each other to obtain spouses. He also provided a line of succession (through Atitapwin) for his material assets and for the initiation partner he had inherited from Waipisi. A wider reorganization, such as the absorption of the truncated partnership into another partnership couplet, was thereby forestalled. A potential empty "cell" resulting from To'ongolal's childlessness was thus filled by the adoption of Atitapwin.

Adoption solves an immediate problem for the senior men involved. But it is also clear from the Waipisi case that adoption helps to preserve the numerical symmetry on which the dual organization depends. In other words, we do not need to look to ritual equilibration as the prime *motive* for adoption. The reasons a man adopts an heir are largely tied to his personal self-interest: security in old age, honor and propitiation after death, and an even sex ratio among his children so as to facilitate their marriages. A consequence of this adoption pattern is a shuffling of children that enables both the marriage system and the initiation system to work. Application of the principles "every man should have a male heir" and "every person should have an opposite-sexed sibling," solves the demographic problem and, *as a consequence*, equilibrates the ritual system at the level of initiation partnerships.

There are important theoretical lessons to be drawn from the case of Ilahita adoption dynamics. First, actions taken by individuals for immediate, self-interested reasons can have incidental, sustaining effects on higher-level, collective structures. Second, if novel circumstances cause a change in the pattern of those individual actions, this would eventually produce changes in the higher-level structures. In this way, higher levels of structure (e.g. initiation moieties and submoieties) *emerge from* lower levels of patterned behavior (e.g. adoption practices). Third, although structural values, once established, may feed back upon and affect behavioral choices, their salience is typically not very great: removing the initiation structures would have little effect on adoption behavior, whereas removing adoption would have a disastrous effect on the initiation structures. Finally, the emergence of formal structures from patterned, "grassroots" behaviors accounts for the orderliness of, directionality of – even the seeming "intelligence" of – social-evolutionary change, despite its non-teleological character.[15]

Turning vinegar into honey

No matter how elegant their social structures may be, residential communities, to survive, require mechanisms for dealing with conflict that arises from time to time. In traditional New Guinea, with its lack of formal law-enforcement agencies and stable political hierarchies, the solution to this problem often entails informal mediation by respected elders, customary compensation payments, peer pressure in support of amity in the group, and the like. Among the Ilahita Arapesh, such measures are used; but the institution *par excellence* for resolving interpersonal conflicts without recourse to physical violence is yam competition. The success of these contests, and the passions which inflame them, have to do with the intense masculine symbolism of this remarkable vegetable (Chapter 2; see also Tuzin 1972). Competition is based on the quantity of yams produced by the individual or group, and/or on the size of individual tubers planted using special techniques and magical aids. Such contests may occur between groups in the village – village moieties, wards, ward moieties – but in this illustration I discuss only competition between individuals.

Because of the symbolic – indeed "phallic" – potency of long yams, competition with these monster tubers is seen as too "hot," too dangerous, between individuals of the same ward. Their main arena is between elements of competing wards or, preferably, between enemy villages. Nevertheless, intense aggressive feelings can arise within the ward, and in this sphere the majority of observed conflicts occurred between ward moieties. It is my impression that conflict *within* the ward moiety is treated as a "family affair" where resolution is attempted within the moralistic frame of reference applicable to relations between close neighbors and kin. Conflict between individuals and groups in different ward moieties takes on a public character; it affects the ward as a whole and causes men to align themselves with their own ward moieties. It must be recalled that ward moieties are residentially separated, a factor contributing to ritual conventions stressing moderate suspiciousness and competition between them.

Hypothetical example: veiled aggression

In order to strike symbolically at a foe in the opposite ward moiety of one's own ward, an individual initiates the protracted chain of events shown in Figure 5. The diagram shows the relevant parties according to their membership in the three dual structures described in the last chapter. The transaction occurs in two phases, the offering and the return. In each phase are shown two wards, directly opposed across the village-moiety division, Laongol versus Bandangel, shown as a vertical line. This could represent, for example, the wards of Balanga and Ililip. The horizontal line divides both wards into their two ward moieties, Afa'afa'w and Ondondof. Within each quadrant is an initiation partnership, Sahopwas (S) and Owapwas (O).

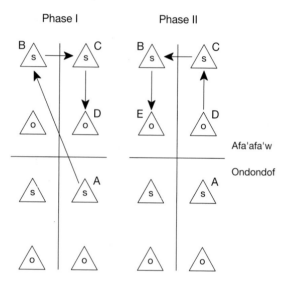

Figure 5 Veiled yam competition

Let us suppose that man A has a grievance against man D who belongs to the opposite ward moiety of A's own ward. A waits until he has a good long yam ready for harvest. He conceals its existence from everyone except his closest confidants; indeed, the prospect of using one's long yam in the manner about to be described is one reason for the secrecy surrounding long-yam cultivation in the first place. When A's yam is harvested he carries it secretly to man B, who is the particular ritual "enemy" (*nautamana*) of man C.[16] This transfer would have been prearranged between A and B, on the basis of what they recognize as a ritual "friendship" (Chapter 6).

The day after B receives the yam from A, he presents it to C, ostensibly because they are ritual competitors who intermittently exchange long yams. It is presented as though B himself had harvested it, and C has no reason to assume otherwise. As anticipated in A's original scheme, C in turn presents the yam to his initiation partner, the man for whom the yam was intended in the first place. Neither C nor D knows that it is A who is seeking to humiliate them.[17]

The return is made to the Laongol middleman at such time as either C or D produces a comparably sized yam. (It would have been one of the conditions of D in accepting the yam to eat that he would not be solely responsible for making the return.) This yam is given to B who passes it on to E for consumption. Note that the return yam does not proceed all the way back to A. This is, in effect, out of recognition by B that A provided the means for his scoring a public victory over his ritual "enemy" at no cost to himself. A's reward is the satisfying discomfiture of his personal enemy, with the secret knowledge that he, A, is the cause of it.

Two general observations about yam exchanges. First, it might appear, in theory, that a returned yam of comparable or superior size converts the earlier disgrace into a victory. In practice this is not so, for until the recipient group makes its return – and this may take a couple of years – they are in a state of humility and ritual inferiority. Their eventual return of a yam removes this stigma, but it does not thereby shift humiliation to the group that initiated the exchange. The net prestige gain is, therefore, won by the group that first gives the yam to its opponent. Because the ritual opposition is ongoing and institutionalized, groups (or individuals) initiate exchanges whenever possible lest the opponent preempt them. In the exchange figured above, the public victory was B's, the private victory was A's, and the defeat fell to C and D.

The other general point is that competitive cycles such as the one illustrated may be several years in duration, and a man might well be involved in more than one at a time. This means that at any given time the community contains many ongoing exchanges at various stages of completion. In fact, these exchanges are often never "complete" in the view of the participants; for, unless the identities of the parties are eventually revealed, a man can never be sure who attacked him. The result is an atmosphere more or less constantly charged with suspicion; but, again, from the community's standpoint, this is far preferable to open, uncontrolled conflict.

The notion that an enemy in one's own ward can be attacked via ritual allies in another ward occurs also in the reported behavior of sorcerers. Following a yam exchange around 1948 between the Ondondof ward moieties of Ililip and Balanga, there was a series of deaths in each ward. In discussing the episode with Ililip informants I was startled at their casual

Plate 33 Aggressive yam competitions occur between, as well as within, villages. Here, two of many long yams from Ilahita are about to be thrust onto the shoulders of representatives from the enemy village of Lehinga. Concealed in the underbrush, scores or hundreds of armed men stand ready in case one of the yams falls and breaks, triggering a fight.

remark that Ililip men probably supplied Balanga sorcerers with the personal leavings (hair or fingernail clippings, spittle, sweat, and the like) of the victims. Why, I asked, would an Ililip man betray his own group to the enemy? They replied that in such cases it is right and proper that certain men in both groups feel aggrieved at the humiliation of their "friends" in the other ward (Harrison 1993: 65). Such feelings lead them to supply the sorcerers of the other group with the means of destruction. This is done along ward-moiety lines, so that an Ililip Afa'afa'w sends the leavings of an Ililip Ondondof to an Ondondof sorcerer in Balanga. If the man receiving the items is not himself a sorcerer, he sees to it that they are passed on to someone knowing the proper magic. The name of the Ililip traitor remains a secret between himself and the man with whom he made contact in the other ward.

The integrative effects of these practices are plain to see. The existence of structured associations outside his ward enables a person to attack or humiliate a fellow wardsman secretly and by indirect means. This is not to say he must do it this way: direct and overt yam contests and sorcery occasionally occur between individuals in a ward. These events, however, run the risk of generalizing the conflict along kinship and neighborhood lines, the consequences of which could be serious disaffection of parts of the ward. By channeling the attack through the circuitous route described above, personal aggressive impulses achieve satisfaction without severe consequences for ward solidarity and harmony.

For present purposes, it is significant that these inter-ward associations are based on the dual organization. There is no logical reason why this must be so: other types of relationship, founded on kinship, marriage, or informal friendship, could have been used. But those alternatives would not have worked nearly as well. For one thing, persons who have neither kinsmen nor friends outside their ward would be unable to use such conventions, undermining their utility from the start. More to the point, if one or a combination of the other relationship types were activated in this aggressive context, the effect would be to extend hostilities outside their ward of origin, encompassing other wards and directly endangering the integration of the village. This is because, as we have seen, individual wards are large enough to survive on their own if they become sufficiently alienated from the rest of the village.

By contrast, the virtue of the dual organization is that, in addition to giving every adult male one or more "friends" and "enemies" in another ward, it *prescribes under controlled conditions* a relationship of competition between paired ward moieties in opposed moieties, but never between wards as wholes. The yam contests between these parties do not, therefore, threaten a breakdown in their ritual relationship. Rather, the reverse: being prescribed within the total system of oppositions, these contests paradoxically *reinforce* the ritual ties and thereby react favorably on village solidarity.

Just as the placing of predictably rivalrous brothers into different initiation moieties ritualizes in socially positive ways the tension between them, so the placing of antagonistic wards into opposite village moieties regulates conflicts arising between them from time to time. Moreover, a significant proportion (by my estimate) of inter-ward symbolic aggression originates from interpersonal antagonisms occurring *within* the ward, arising from the combination of hot tempers and residential proximity. Finally, by enlisting the aid of the opposite ward moiety of the "enemy" ward, and providing them with a public victory over members of one's own ward, the effect is to provide a motivational component to the ritual interdependency prescribed by the dual organization. This is in addition to the operation of the Tambaran itself, the massive works of which demand cooperation between all parts of the village (see above).

In sum, in addition to the reinforcing exercises given them by the Tambaran, the system of dual structures in Ilahita depends in large part on input received from interpersonal and inter-group antagonism. Without this input, ritually prescribed behavior would probably wither away, for it would cease to bear any functional relation to actual behavior. As history proved, this did not happen. Instead, aggressive interactions continued within the village, but without the overarching necessity (in the interests of military security) for their containment or sublimation. As the Tambaran began to weaken during the middle 1970s, contests become raw and irresolvable, increasingly causing disgruntled parties to remove to Ilahita's hinterland, or to leave the area entirely.

These post-pacification, post-Tambaran developments verify the functional workings of the dual organization as it existed during Ilahita's period of greatness. That is to say, a well-articulated system of conventions for ritualized competition managed aggression in ways that were not only not disruptive, they positively contributed to the cohesion of the ritual system. That function was served all the way from the lowest structural level of fraternal rivalry to the sphere of inter-ward and village-moiety relations on which depended the solidarity, military power, and viability of the entire village.

Conclusion

Sometime around the third quarter of the nineteenth century, the preda-tory incursion of Abelam groups into the foothill region brought about a significant expansion of Ilahita's population and radically altered, both internally and externally, its "environment of adaptedness" (Bowlby 1971: 72). Unprecedented, chronic military threat required defensible villages – the larger, the better – which is why Ilahita leaders of the time were inclined to receive rather than repel refugee groups that appeared at their door. But larger settlements could not be sustained without integrative structures of greater compass than those achievable by primordial relations of kinship and descent. New relationship structures were needed, so to speak, to bridge the non-kinship space created when independent groups came together in residential proximity.

The model seized upon was simplicity itself and in some form was adopted from the Abelam themselves: a dual organization in which population growth was accommodated through progressive structural sub-division and ritual integration. Whether by internal growth or accretion, as units became too unwieldy to cooperate in the tasks assigned to them, they subdivided, and the new dual opposition thus formed was given a domain of interaction all its own. The result was an exquisitely complex and resilient system of mechanical solidarity: a system of contrived inter-dependency, which maintained the units in positive relationship with one another, while absorbing and dissipating pressures that otherwise would have led to the dissolution of the village.[18] And as the village grew, so did the mechanical complexity of its dual organization, enabling additional growth and correspondingly enhanced military and diplomatic prosperity.

Along with the dual organization came a ritual system well suited to this new and hostile environment: the Tambaran – an Abelam cult that gloried in war and human sacrifice, produced stupendous works of ritual art and architecture, and exalted masculinity while excluding and denigrating women. Indications are that the Abelam cult was grafted on to a pre-existing Arapesh system of initiation that carried males (and possibly females) only to adolescence. Nggwal Bunafunei, the tambaran of *warriors*, originated as a product of Abelam imagination. Subsequently, however, Ilahita's size enabled it to populate an independent grade of cult *elders*, Nggwal Walipeine. This innovation effectively centralized village authority on a ritual basis and laid the groundwork for the emergence of a rationalized religious ethic, following the cessation of endemic warfare. All of these – the ideas, practices, and rankings of the Tambaran cult, along with the complex, secular workings of the dual organization – were the social and cultural key to Ilahita's success as an immense village.

During the period of history covered in this study, Ilahita's environment of adaptedness received several major jolts. As just recalled, there was the Abelam advent in the nineteenth century, which brought hazards and opportunities that decisively shaped the village's future development. Secondly, with initial White contact early in the twentieth century, Ilahita's universe suddenly included radically different kinds of people. In addition to the specific experiences of colonial governance, labor recruitment, and missionization, the increasing awareness of other racial types and other ways of behaving gave a new level of cultural self-consciousness to the village. With this cognitive change, the Ilahita Arapesh became more acutely aware of their separate identity, as embodied in traditional beliefs and practices. Because it influenced so many areas of sociocultural life, the Tambaran became the champion and proxy for that tradition, especially when the competing doctrine of mission Christianity arrived on the scene. Indeed, by the 1950s the Tambaran had become the personified mystique of a total way of life, and traditionalists came to be called "Tambaran men."

The third major change was the cessation of warfare, which nominally occurred in 1944, with the Japanese military occupation, and was finally achieved around 1952. In this study I have emphasized the importance of large-scale, endemic warfare as a factor – indeed, the constitutional factor – in Ilahita's growth and lasting integrity (cf. Carneiro 1970). The removal of that factor did not have immediate effects, but in the long run it proved to be the beginning of the end of Ilahita as a unified village. The structures and mechanisms that arose in response to the early emergency circumstances of war were no longer viable when the emergency had passed. The divisive pressures that once had to be contained no longer needed to be. Today, those pressures are being further exacerbated by a population explosion brought about by recently improved medical and hygiene conditions. Disaffected groups are no longer deterred from dispersing into the village's hinterland, and that is precisely what they are doing. History appears to be coming full circle, though of course the circle never ends precisely where it began. The dismantling of Ilahita may be tantamount to culture "seeking its own level" – a reversion, in that the settlement pattern now taking shape is not dissimilar from the one that prevailed before the Abelam arrived on the scene. But the social circumstances, both internal and external to the village, are vastly different now to what they were when the circle began. The problem of bringing cultural values and social practices into alignment is the challenge now facing the people of Ilahita. It is a challenge not unique to themselves, but is one that has faced humanity since culture began; it is the price we pay for being human in the social mode.

8   Conclusion

The Greek philosopher Heraclitus is famous for having said, "One cannot step into the same river twice." Change is incessant in human life, if only because no day is identical to another, and no generation does things exactly the way its parents did. Social systems reduce the chaos by containing change within customary limits and by imposing reliable, legally or morally enforceable, understandings and expectations on human behavior. Only when change accumulates and becomes integrated with other parts of the system, and begins to alter the understandings and expectations themselves, is it useful to speak of the process as "evolutionary." Furthermore, just as biological evolution relies on random genetic mutations, so social evolution is fueled by minute changes of human perception, experience, and behavior, resulting in individual and collective actions whose long-term cumulative effects, while not random, are almost always impossible to predict in advance.

This book is an *evolutionary* history of Ilahita village over the last century and a half, a span covering a succession of transformational phases. The Pre-Tambaran was the period of the ancestral culture, before the fateful intrusion of the Abelam, before the men's cult took charge of the village on a major scale. The Tambaran period, between approximately 1870 and 1950, was the era of dramatic population growth, sociocultural efflorescence, initial contact with Whites, and the lordly success of Ilahita in the local region. Late Tambaran began with the final cessation of endemic warfare in 1950 and concluded with the coming of national independence in 1975. This was the period during which "modern" influences increasingly penetrated village life: the Mission, the cash economy, democratic political institutions, village courts, and European-style education. The Tambaran cult remained strong and feared, but, as with the elders who ruled through it, its power was slowly draining away. The Post-Tambaran period culminated with the 1984 revelation of cult secrets to the women and the corresponding collapse of the dual organization, the masculine mystique, and all objects and practices associated with the Tambaran.

As an evolutionary account of these historical stages and the transitions between them, the study pursued three interwoven strands: (1) the structures and processes of social life, including the ways in which those elements reproduce themselves; (2) perturbations coming from outside the village's sociocultural boundaries; and (3) the system-altering effects of (2) on (1). This last is important, because it addresses the crucial issue of adaptive *mechanisms*. It is not enough to say that changes occurred, or to identify successive stages of development, or to observe that village society went from being simple to being complex, or to say that village population and social complexity increased together. Rather, to be "evolutionary" in any meaningful sense, an analysis must identify elements of absorptiveness, resilience, and brittleness in the native system; features akin to selection and fittedness in terms of the choices people make; the structural consequences of those choices in aggregate; and, withal, the precise circumstances under which novelty emerges and is incorporated.

Most of the elements in this history are singular: the society and culture of Ilahita are unique, though they bear a "family resemblance" to systems found elsewhere; also, the details of what has happened in and to the village comprise a unique communal biography. At a more general level of abstraction, however, several of Ilahita's sociocultural transformations exemplify those that have been repeated (with pertinent cultural variations) at many times and in many places in world history. Taken together, these transitions are *dimensional* aspects of the movement from simpler, small-scale societies to more complex, large-scale societies.

We are speaking here not of clearly definable types or categories of societies but of recursive phases, gradients of relative emphasis, and complex features encompassing, rather than replacing, simpler ones. I recall as a newcomer to Tokyo being surprised that this vast, bustling, modern metropolis is actually composed of thousands of tiny neighborhoods: intimate, face-to-face communities, many quite old, where everyone knows everyone else, and where shopkeeper–customer relationships go back sometimes for generations. In Tokyo's growth and modernization, simplicity had not gone away, but had become nestled within additional structures of overarching size and complexity. With the proviso, then, that complex forms often subsume older, simpler forms, let us review the major transitions exemplified in the Ilahita case (Table 7).

In societal terms, scale normally implies size. As an adaptation to a growing resident population, Ilahita society in the Tambaran period increased in scale, which is to say, the structures and processes of social action multiplied in step with the expanding number of people living in this sedentary, highly nucleated village. And vice versa: without the evolution of structures and processes to accommodate this population

Table 7 Major sociocultural transitions

Small scale	>>>>>	Large scale
Collectivism	>>	Individualism
Kinship	>>	Citizenship
Gift exchange	>>	Commodity exchange
Multiplex relationships	>>	Simplex relationships
Egalitarianism	>>	Hierarchy
Amoral magicality	>>	Religious ethic

growth, it would not have happened. Ilahita, like other settlements throughout New Guinea, would have stayed relatively small; overall population growth in the region, were it to have occurred, would have been more widely and evenly dispersed.

Archaeologists and cultural historians are quick to point to factors of increasing size and sedentism of populations as conditions for the rise of cities in the ancient Near East and other early civilizational centers (e.g. Childe 1950; Wittfogel 1957; Harris 1977). With so much of sociocultural process missing from the archaeological record, however, one must necessarily presuppose that mechanisms of integration emerged early in the game, long before bureaucracies, royal palaces and libraries, and other stately achievements arose and left physical traces of themselves. As an indication of such early integration, temples with monumental carved pillars and sculptures appear in the archaeological record in the pre-pottery Neolithic period, in the late eighth to middle seventh millennia BC, thousands of years before the rise of literate states (Hauptmann 1993, 1999; also Yoffee 1993: 70). The Ilahita case shows, in some ethnographic detail, how societal scale and population dynamics might interact at an early stage of organizational complexity; how temples might *sponsor* settlement growth and political integration, not merely result from them.

In this evolutionary account, we observe what can happen when local populations increase beyond the integrative capacity of kinship-based groups. If the community is to stay together, the suprakinship "space" created by the coming-together of unrelated groups must be structured in some way. Descent groups such as clans, by linking people on the basis of what we might call "virtual kinship," effectively extend the "reach" of kinship and its axiom of amity into that unstructured, uncharted space. Ilahita clans function in this manner. Going beyond this, clanship and kinship both provide metaphors for larger, more encompassing structures that pick up, so to speak, where clans leave off. The dual organization is drenched with kinship and descent significance, even though the parties integrated through it are usually unrelated. Through those metaphors, the system extends primordial meaning into these new areas, and in the process gives them authenticity and legitimacy.

While Ilahita's dual organization is a dazzling example of mechanical social solidarity, various evidence suggests that it is likely to have been an elaboration of an older, Pre-Tambaran pattern of group reciprocity, probably one based on bilateral marriage exchange. Nothing we know suggests that the logic of the village's dual organization was entirely novel – either as acquired from the Abelam or as it developed internally in response to Abelam influences. Nor is there reason to infer from the Ilahita case that mechanical systems naturally evolve into organic systems, or are always and everywhere a precursor of them; hence the omission of this transition from Table 7. Instead, it would appear that mechanical systems proceed from a different logic – one leading, ultimately, into evolutionary blind alleys.

The reason is that mechanical systems have severe integrative limitations, beyond which they become unwieldy. Ilahita in the heyday of its Tambaran period may have been pushing at those limits. Even as I observed Late Tambaran social life to be humming along quite nicely, I could not conceive the village and its dual organization continuing to grow larger and more complex without becoming unstuck, as it eventually did. This is a far cry from the open-ended, sky's-the-limit quality of social evolution in the organic mode. Accordingly, Ilahita's transition to "modernity" appears to have occurred not by the release of some previously unexploited potential in the traditional system, but by a traumatic breakdown of its mechanical elements and a "restarting" of the system along organic lines.[1]

That is certainly how the men saw it. The staged, hugely symbolic killing of the Tambaran was the most dramatic way they knew to say it: the Past is finished; let the Future begin. But revolutions always seem more radical at the time than they do in retrospect. Only time and the next equilibrium will tell whether that break between past and future was as sharp as the men intended it to be.

Wherever Ilahita's final future may lie, the Late Tambaran period witnessed major changes which were probably rendered irreversible by the killing of the Tambaran. Recalling Table 7, these changes may be summarized as rocky transitions from:

- *collectivism to individualism*, principally in the areas of property ownership, marriage transactions, legal responsibility, and social identity;

- *kinship to citizenship*, as a person's social and legal identity became decreasingly dictated by kinship, descent, and ritual-class considerations, but by the state of Papau New Guinea and its organs;
- *gift exchange to commodity exchange*, as relationships that were formerly infused with moral obligations, such as sister-exchange marriage and resource distribution, became reduced to quasi-commercial cash transactions; and
- *multiplex relationships to simplex relationships*, as modern conditions enabled villagers to interact with strangers in practical, unidimensional contexts.

One does not have to revert to discredited nineteenth-century Evolutionism or to the fixed typological sequencing of recent Neo-Evolutionism to observe that, in all of these transitions, Ilahita's experience is the story-writ-small of most human societies. In time, it *will* be universal – not in speculative theory, but in accomplished fact.

Given that mechanical systems of social solidarity are composed of relatively equivalent parts, it follows, almost by definition, that they are associated with egalitarian ideology, and that the failure of one entails the failure of the other. For Americans at least, "egalitarianism" has a gentle Jeffersonian ring to it, evoking images of ruggedly decent, buckskin-clad pioneers working together in harmony for the good of one and all. The truth is actually quite the opposite: egalitarianism is typically a rather savage doctrine, for it involves constant vigilance and intrigue among society's members as they struggle to stay equal to each other. Competition, not harmony, is the hallmark of egalitarian systems; gossip, envy, jealousy, and accusations of sorcery are endemic to them. One could even interpret Ilahita's dual organization during the Tambaran and Late Tambaran periods as a mechanism that relieved, but was also a product of, the stresses engendered by egalitarianism under conditions where disputants could no longer go their own ways (cf. Rappaport 1968; Forge 1972b: 533–4; Johnson 1982).

Elsewhere in the world, principles of hierarchy and organic solidarity may have been co-evolutionary partners from a very early stage in the movement to large-scale societies. Evidence from Cro-Magnon burials "hint[s] at a social stratification and division of labor" going back as much as 28,000 years (Tattersall 1998: 12). In a scenario quite different from Ilahita's, one could easily imagine some local leader rising to prominence and, by a combination of conquest, charm, and strategic alliances, extending his or her sway well beyond the circle of kinship, clanship, even beyond the ethnic group. Over time, such a beginning could lead to the kinds of organically elaborate city-states that arose in the ancient Near East and in other cradles of civilization. To be sure, hierarchy has worries of its own, the prospect of palace or popular revolt being the most obvious among them. But the expectations and understandings that hierarchy engenders can also be quite stable; folks on the lower rungs *can* be content with their lot and supportive of a morality that places them there (Parish 1996: 201–2). Like it or not, hierarchy's inherent potential for wealth, power, and authority to be concentrated in a few hands has been the green light on the road to societal complexity.

This brings us to the last and perhaps most remarkable of Ilahita's transformations: the centralizing of ritual authority in a designated class of Tambaran elders, and their coordinated use of that authority to control people's behavior – an innovation that appears to have reached final form during the Late Tambaran period. Everywhere it is found, hierarchy ultimately appeals to superhuman forces to justify and empower itself. African, Asian, and European divine-right kingship – the anointing of the king as God's chosen ruler – is a pure example of this idea; the Laws of Manu, which, in Hindu teachings, are the revelations of Brahman in decreeing India's hierarchically ordered society, is another; national politics in the United States has always been replete with references to heavenly intention. In Ilahita, the village population grew large enough to permit the creation of a viable cult rank occupied by the old men. Claiming special knowledge vouchsafed to them by ancestral and cult spirits, the elders identified themselves as custodians not simply of this or that *tambaran*, but of a transcendent, unitary Tambaran that was the champion of the village and the personified mystique of Tradition.

Prior to this innovation, the spirit realm was a projection of the mechanical ordering and egalitarian ethos of mortals: an array of structurally identical sets of ancestral and cult spirits, each associated with a particular clan. Through magical manipulation by their human clients, the spirits competed, just as men did, and there was no articulated higher morality to which all were subordinate. Manifesting a kind of amoral magicality, the arrangement amounted to an uneasy alliance among the village's cult spirits.

The emergence of the transcendent Tambaran projected not this array of equivalent spirits, but a *unified* spiritual force that patronized *the village* and operated through the decrees of old men. Their personal interests mutually coincided far more than at an earlier time in their political careers. Thus, the unified Tambaran can also be viewed as a projection of the transcendent unity of its worldly custodians, the old men of Nggwal Walipeine. Under the influences of rising population, the cessation of warfare, and novel threats to the authority of the old men, a qualitatively new *hierarchical* concept was fashioned from pre-existing cultic ideas and structures. Conduct became subject to a rationalized religious ethic – judged and punished according to Tambaran precepts proclaimed by the cult elders. Because of the ensuing death of the Tambaran and the dismantling of the dual organization, it is impossible to know to what new social formations that ethical development might have led. But we can say that, for a brief evolutionary moment, within the span of a generation living in the twilight of Ilahita's greatness, a system that had worked so well in the past but whose world was changing, yet again, seemed ready to try something truly new.

Notes

1 Introduction

1 The crusade against nineteenth-century evolutionism was widely subscribed and was led by Franz Boas (e.g. Boas 1896), the man who "founded" American cultural anthropology at about the turn of the twentieth century. The anti-evolutionist passion that prevailed for virtually the entire first half of the twentieth century is expressed in the words of a Boasian, Berthold Laufer, writing in 1918: "The theory of cultural evolution [is] to my mind the most inane, sterile, and pernicious theory in the whole theory of science" (quoted in White 1960: v). It would be thirty years before Neo-Evolutionism and other revisionist approaches would take up problems of social evolution. Even to this day, many social and cultural anthropologists remain wary of evolutionary questions, believing, quite unfairly, that such inquiry is inherently racist and ethnocentric. For a fascinating study that answers this scholarly prejudice head-on, see Diamond (1997). As examples of other recent works that are unapologetic about asking important questions concerning social evolution, see Johnson and Earle (1987) and Feil (1987).

2 In Elman Service's original formulation (Service 1962), this type was labeled "tribes." Ambiguities surrounding this term, along with an amount of unwanted intellectual baggage, have prompted most scholars to shift to the more accurate and descriptive phrase "segmentary societies." In his discussions of the rise of chiefdoms, Robert Carneiro (1981, 1991) terms this prior type "autonomous village societies."

3 Norman Yoffee is a vigorous critic of Neo-Evolutionism, the archaeological camp that has particularly embraced the typological method I am discussing. The "taxonomic labels of neo-evolutionism," Yoffee writes (1993: 72), "have falsely ranked the diversity of human societies, both past and present. These labels have also been wrongly used by archaeologists who seek to 'type' a prehistoric society as a 'state' or a 'chiefdom' as if such a categorization might elevate their empirical research into the realm of higher evolutionary thought – and as if they actually know something more about a prehistoric society having so stuck a label on it."

This is harsh language. Although, as will be seen, I have criticisms of my own, especially as regards the application of typological reasoning to evolutionary processes, I would hope that Yoffee is not advocating the abolition of typologies *in principle*. Taxonomies are *made* to be criticized, *made* to be improved upon or overturned in favor of a superior way of organizing our thoughts about reality; that is what we call "progress" in scientific inquiry. If used judiciously – that is, not crediting them with a concreteness, permanence, or explanatory power they do not possess – taxonomies can be important, quite valid elements in the wider methodology.

4 Among the many works which exemplify, modify, or criticize typological approaches to social evolution, those I have found to be especially illuminating are Steward (1955); Sahlins and Service (1960); Service (1962); Sanders and Price (1968); Sanders and Marino (1970); Fried (1967); Carneiro (1970); M. Harris (1977); Cohen and Service (1978); D.R. Harris (1994); Johnson and Earle (1987); Yoffee (1993); Flannery (1994, 1999); and Trigger (1998). For a refreshingly different approach, one that examines factors of environment, geography, and the domesticability of various wild plants and animals to explain why social complexity arose in, or diffused to, different parts of the world at quite different times, see Diamond (1997).

5 Ian Tattersall (1998: 86) makes a similar point with regard to the difficulty of imagining the precise moment of speciation, when parent and offspring oddly belong to different species. At the root of all evolutionary typologies is the paradox of the self-transcending type. The way out of this conundrum is to admit that typologies, as such, are not evolutionary at all.

6 The model I am proposing bears likeness to the powerful idea of "punctuated equilibria," as developed in palaeontology (Gould and Eldredge 1977; Tattersall 1998). Elsewhere, I have used the idea of "pre-existing potential" to analyze the relationship between leadership types (Tuzin 1991) and between partner traditions of belief and skepticism in ideological systems (Tuzin 1980: 312–16).

7 A glossary of recurring technical and vernacular terms is appended to this volume.

8 The exclusion of women does not prevent the men from securing *feminine* involvement, however, which is essential for the procreative purposes of the rituals. This is achieved, surreptitiously, by purveying to the women rather far-fetched claims of what the men supposedly do in their secret conclaves. Unbeknown to the women, these claims are veiled renditions of the truth of the ritual proceedings. For example, with reference to Lefin grade rites, where boys are cleansed of maternal blood essences by having their penises slashed, the women are told that the youths are made to slide down thorny sago palms (a maternal symbol), ripping their bellies open. Other claims, such as that adolescent Maolimu-grade initiates in seclusion are transformed into giant fruit bats, are even more fantastical. By acquiescing to these fictions – "belief" would be too strong a term for their attitude – the women unwittingly lend their femininity to the men's endeavors. For more on this symbolic maneuver and its underlying cultural psychology, see Tuzin (1995).

9 By the time of my first field work (1969–72), Melanesian Pidgin (MP) was spoken by virtually all men under 40 and all women under 30; no villager spoke English. By the mid-1980s, MP fluency had become nearly universal in the village, and a good many young people had acquired basic English in school. My proficiency in the difficult Arapesh language enabled me to carry on simple conversations and to catch the gist of what people within earshot were saying to each other; but true fluency eluded me, and much of my field work was carried out in Melanesian Pidgin or with the help of MP-speaking interpreters.

2 The setting

1 In a fascinating study of social evolution in the New Guinea highlands, Feil (1987) perceives a gradient of development in productive resources running from west to east. The western area, he argues, developed intensified agriculture and pig husbandry very much earlier than the eastern, which had a mixed economy of horticulture and hunting until the introduction of the sweet potato – ultimately from the Portuguese – only a few hundred years ago. From this historical difference flows a broad spectrum of sociocultural variations among Highlands societies, west to east, following the same gradient.

2 At the time of the Last Glacial Maximum, about 18,000 years ago, low sea-levels formed New Guinea, Australia, and Tasmania into a continuous landmass, which scientists call "Sahul." A deep-water trench west of New Guinea, known as the Wallace Line, formed a diffusion barrier that isolated the marsupial mammals of Sahul and prevented placental mammals from colonizing the region. It is presumed that placental mammals found in traditional New Guinea (dogs, pigs, and rats) were brought there by humans, who, over 50,000 years ago, devised watercraft capable of carrying them across the Wallace Line. Bats, the only other placental mammal, probably got to New Guinea on their own.

New Guinea, it may be mentioned, is one of the few places on earth to have developed agriculture independently, as early as 7000 BC (Diamond 1997: 148).

3 The name "Arapesh" refers to a family of at least three languages inhabiting this general region, of which "Southern Arapesh" is one. "Ilahita Arapesh" is one of three dialects of Southern Arapesh. See Map 2.

4 By contrast, "intensive" systems are those which depend on natural (e.g. riverine flooding) or artificial (e.g. use of chemicals or compost) refertilization of the land on a frequent – usually annual – basis, enabling the farmer every year to cultivate the same plot of land.

5 Such reasons could be human population increase under, say, improved health and hygiene conditions, or, on the other side of the ratio, the loss of arable land due to environmental alterations or alternative uses, such as ranching, mining, or cash-cropping; or, as has happened in Ilahita in recent decades, both population increase and land loss.

6 When it comes to garden exotics, the Ilahita are willing to try anything; but their palates are conservative, and they usually end up not liking new foods or considering them not worth the trouble. Some such products, which are still planted in small quantities by some families, are: sweet potato and cassava, which were introduced by Japanese troops during World War II; pineapple, green beans, and tomato, which were introduced during the 1950s by Christian missionaries; and peanuts, which were introduced by Australian agricultural officers during the 1960s in an unsuccessful attempt to establish them as a cash crop.

7 A non-sweet, cooking banana.

8 Tobacco was domesticated in the New World, and in many Native American cultures it is an important ritual substance. In New Guinea, this is generally not the case, probably because of tobacco's relative recency. In Ilahita, men smoke long slender cigarettes, rolled in tobacco leaves or, more prestigiously, pages from the *Sydney Morning Herald*, which are available by the sheet at exorbitant prices in local trade stores. Women roll tobacco into fat, day-long cigars, which, curiously, they smoke *with the lit end in their mouths.*

9 From the mid-1970s, as income from coffee, cacao, and remittances sent by persons working for wages outside the village steadily grew, cash began to have a noticeable effect on dietary practices. Rice and tinned fish were more frequently consumed than before, store-bought meats (chicken, beef, mutton tongue, etc.) were available at shops in the local district headquarters of Maprik, and beer-drinking became a favorite pastime of young men. These changes corresponded with increased mobility, as commercial vehicles competed to carry goods and passengers along the Sepik Highway, an all-weather road which connects Wewak, Maprik and points west, and which passes about 11 kilometers to the north of Ilahita.

10 Strictly speaking, these are *feral* pigs, since they were presumably domesticated at the time, long ago, when humans brought them to New Guinea. Male pigs born in the village are castrated at an early age, and domestic female pigs are fertilized by wild males, resulting in a steady genetic communication between wild and village pigs. Belying the tender sentiments lavished on pigs, men dispatch them in a particularly gruesome way, namely, by burning them to death. This mode of execution conveniently removes the pig's stiff body hairs preparatory to butchering and cooking; it also produces horrific shrieks from the unfortunate animal which attract wild pigs closer to the village. So it is said.

11 A fierce, flightless bird that stands as tall as a man (160 centimeters) and is reputed to be the only bird that can "kill a man at one blow" (Burton and Burton 1969: 385) – this by means of a rapier-like talon that it uses to stab or rake the belly of an opponent.

12 A cat-sized, short-legged marsupial rodent.

13 A kind of small kangaroo.

14 Locusts and fledglings are simply pounced upon. For catching lizards, boys use an ingenious technique. With a length of bamboo and a line made of bush materials, the child fashions a "fishing pole," baited with a live locust, which he dangles into the high grass alongside a path. Before the unlucky lizard thinks to relax his bite, he himself is dangling with his mates on the boy's stringer.

15 The gender symbolism of bushy, crooked or meandering as "female," and straight as "male," applies to other plants, rivers and streams, yams, and practically everything else that lends itself to this morphological variation.

16 In one observed case, a palm requiring 74 adult work-hours to process, yielded 111 kilograms of (wet) sago flour, which translated into an estimated yield of 4.7 adult meals for each adult work-hour.

17 The maternal implication of this convergence is elaborated upon in a story in which a pregnant woman finds herself hanging from a cloud. Unable to rescue her, her husband digs a hole underneath where she is suspended. When she dies, her fetus and bodily fluids drop into the hole. Nurtured by his mother's ghost-empowered liquids, the fetus completes his development, emerges from the hole, and eventually grows into a hero with supernatural powers.

18 This danger is the reason why only ritually senior males eat long yams, for they have the spiritual strength to withstand the power of the magic.

19 Long yams are not really grown primarily as food; in any case, they are relatively woody and much less tasty than their short cousins. Ironically, as men will admit, the tastiest yams of all are grown by the women. Barred from piercing the ground with a stick, women plant small yams, by hand, in the piles of sweepings that form accidental compost beds along the margins of the garden.

20 If undamaged and stored properly, yams remain edible for several months. This is due, in part, to the fact that they undergo a physiological dormancy after harvest (Bryant Allen, pers. comm.).

21 Ilahita people say that a child loses his milk teeth because they are "pushed out" by his younger sibling.

22 This is a double-edged, blade-shaped object 20–25 centimeters long, to which is attached a long cord. When the bullroarer is swung at the end of its tether, the sound produced is an eerie humming and whining, which is said to be the "voice" of the spirit associated with this (Lefin) grade. Although each boy is given a bullroarer at the time of initiation, the object itself is kept by the men, lest it be inadvertently seen by women.

23 Do the women actually "believe" such outlandish claims? The short answer, which I obtained only years later, after the Tambaran cult had collapsed, is that the women did not believe such stories as young men turning into flying foxes and fornicating the night away. On the other hand, they did not know what *did* go on in the forest, and, for reasons described in Chapter 7, were afraid to try to find out.

3 History

1 In later life the officer in charge of the patrol, G.W.L. Townsend, published his New Guinea memoirs (Townsend 1968), as did another member of the patrol, J.K. McCarthy (McCarthy 1963), both of whom included accounts of the Gough incident. For readers interested in the swashbuckling days of New Guinea first contact and control, as well as the attitudes of the colonial field officers, both books are recommended.

2 There never was much gold found in the Prince Alexanders; but other parts of New Guinea yielded major quantities, and to this day gold-mining is an important source of the nation's wealth.

3 Details concerning World War II events in Ilahita were obtained from eyewitness reports and from battle diaries and other official documents lodged in the Australian War Archives, Canberra.

4 Despite this implied opposition, during the early period of missionization (c. 1952–69), relations between cult traditionalists and the missionaries were generally cordial, thanks largely to the charitable attitude of Liesbeth Schrader, the head of the station. See Tuzin (1997: ch. 2) for a discussion of those relations.

5 The type of polygamy in which a man takes multiple wives. The opposite form, rare in the world, in which a woman takes multiple husbands, is known as "polyandry."

6 Self-objectification is a feature of all cultural groups, to some extent, insofar as they perceive their ideas and customs to be different from those of other known groups. This process, which Theodore Schwartz (1975) calls "cultural totemism," has gone very far throughout New Guinea, in step with the amazing proliferation of self-identified cultural and linguistic groups. Accordingly, the process being described for Ilahita was an extension of a mode of cultural cognition very old and widespread in the region.

7 Around this period, "revival movements" were springing up all over New Guinea. Although Ilahitans knew of, and were inspired by, some of the other movements, the version they produced was all their own, and the village

quickly became a center of Revivalist activities, attracting pilgrims from all over this part of the Sepik region.
8 The full story of this event and its aftermath is told in Tuzin (1997).
9 It may be thought that this system could equally be called "brother exchange," but this would violate the Arapesh sense of it, which is that men stay in their place, and women move. In some respects, a more accurate phrasing would be "daughter exchange," insofar as it is the fathers who typically make these arrangements while the marriage candidates are still children. Such a usage, however, would unfortunately imply that the fathers are marrying each other's daughters. In general, it is advisable to stay with the accepted convention and call the practice "sister exchange."
10 The advent of brideprice practices is another step in what will later be described as the movement from "prescriptive" to "proscriptive" marriage systems (Chapter 6).

4 How Ilahita got big

1 Such evidence must be used cautiously, however, for some New Guinea groups are known to have changed languages quite readily. See Filer (1990) for a critique of the use of language boundaries to reconstruct cultural affinities and population movements.
2 Mead (1938) does describe hereditary "paths" through the Prince Alexanders, regular routes linking plainsmen of the interior with exchange partners on the coast. Presumably, such a communication network would have developed only after Arapesh speakers had moved into the mountain and coastal areas, that is, in direct or indirect response to Abelam pressures. What transmontane traffic existed *before* that time, we will probably never know.
3 Two lines of evidence support this interpretation. First, when the Mountain Arapesh were first studied by Margaret Mead in the early 1930s, mountain settlements were sparse and tiny. Soon afterward, in the middle to latter part of that decade, when employment opportunities opened up on the coast and on the New Guinea islands of New Britain and New Ireland, the mountains were virtually vacated, implying a distinctly tenuous attachment to the land. Secondly, although Arapesh speakers live on the coast – Mead calls these the "Beach Arapesh" – they have not developed a maritime economy, and cannot build seaworthy canoes, suggesting a relative recency of habitation there.
4 The motives for this fighting cannot be known in detail; but one likely circumstance is that the Abelam were in turmoil over a self-inflicted land shortage: disorderly retreat before spreading grassfields that they were helping to create through poor slash-and-burn practices (Reiner and Robbins 1964). Once this tough sword grass takes over, the land is good for nothing but periodic burn-offs to drive game.
5 Debate exists over just how peace-loving the Mountain Arapesh actually were. Mead's own data are somewhat contradictory on the matter, suggesting that some amount of inter-group aggression existed that perhaps did not rise to Mead's notion of "warfare." Reo Fortune (1939), Mead's co-worker and then-husband, scathingly criticized this characterization, but in terms that leave the facts somewhat ambiguous. Paul Roscoe (pers. comm.), who has recently worked among the neighboring Boiken people and has spent time among the Mountain Arapesh, is of the opinion that the latter were not the pacifists Mead

made them out to be, and that, if they were, they would have been wiped out long ago by the Boiken. Whatever the truth of the matter, there can be no doubt that the scale, severity, and incessancy of warfare among the "Abelamized" *Ilahita* Arapesh (see text, below) far exceeded any comparable practices among their mountain-dwelling cousins.

6 For example, the two highest grades of the Ilahita Tambaran are called "Nggwal," which is the term used by the Abelam to designate quasi-ancestral cult spirits (*nggwalndu*) and is cognate with the Iatmul term *nggwail*, meaning "grandparent," "grandchild," or "the totemic ancestors of a clan" (Bateson 1936: 310; see Map 1). The three lowest grades of the Ilahita Tambaran are less obviously Abelam in origin, and it is possible that they are modified versions of a pre-existing initiation system, such as exists in other Torricelli societies.

7 Although present-day enmities and alliances go back to a time beyond memory, there is circumstantial evidence that this particular arrangement did not predate the Abelam intrusion, but was a result of disrupted inter-village relationships caused by that intrusion. Indeed, such a view would accord better with the lower-key quality of inter-group hostilities under the ancestral conditions reconstructed above.

8 For a fascinating discussion of differences between the Abelam and the Ilahita Arapesh, in the context of a more detailed treatment, than here, of Abelam predatory expansion, see Forge (1990). See Tuzin (1995) for further treatment of this comparison.

9 In brief (see Tuzin 1997: chs 4 and 5, for details), the story was adopted, indirectly, from Moluccan plume hunters who were active some distance west of Ilahita, or from plantation workers on the coast, during the closing decades of the nineteenth century. Demonstrably a version of the "Swan Maiden" tale that originated in India and spread east and west through much of the Old World, upon reaching Ilahita the story's plot was modified to fit the moral crisis newly affecting the culture at that time.

Now called Maluku, the Moluccas are the fabled Spice Islands, which lie just to the west of New Guinea. For many centuries they operated on the fringes of great Malay trading empires spanning Arabia, India, and China. Bird-of-paradise plumes were among the elite goods that entered this trade; from early in the Christian era, specimens found their way to the Chinese imperial court. For geographical reasons described in Tuzin (1997: ch. 4), during these many centuries Moluccan plume hunters restricted their efforts to the northwestern portions of New Guinea, until after the 1852 founding of Hollandia, when they began to penetrate the coastal mountains of present-day Papua New Guinea. This activity reached its height around the turn of the century, when bird-of-paradise plumes became very popular among fashion-minded European women.

10 Modern scholarship confirms that "warfare, long considered a destroyer of complex societies, was also one of the factors creating complex societies" (Flannery 1994: 105; see also Carneiro 1970; Johnson and Earle 1987; and Harris 1977). The role of warfare as both a destroyer and a creator of social complexity invites comparison with the "punctuations" in the palaeontological record – events which produce the extinction of some species and the prominence of others (e.g. Tattersall 1998: 92–4).

5 Residence structures

1 If small-town America seems more like Ilahita, in important respects it is not; for our local institutions, public and private, are thoroughly integrated with others at regional, state, and national levels – all of which stand ready to assist or direct the locality should the need arise. Traditionally, Ilahita was completely on its own – which, when you think about it, is a sobering idea.

2 It should be noted that pastoralists are typically both very mobile and very war-like, for livestock are a highly stealable kind of property.

3 Domestic or "household" units are those which share economic functions of food-getting and consumption, child care, and the like. In modern Western society, domestic units generally coincide with nuclear families; in kinship-based societies, they typically consist of two or more nuclear families linked by sibling or parent–child ties.

4 Parents encourage adolescent children to establish separate sleeping quarters, for – premarital intercourse being strongly taboo – it is thought that the "hot," unrelieved sexuality of youth could damage the father's gardening and hunting magic. If circumstances force an adolescent child, especially a nubile daughter, to sleep at home, the father usually removes to his nearby yam house.

5 A group constituted of persons related through males, who are termed "agnates." In Ilahita, patrilines are genealogically quite shallow: a set of brothers, their father, paternal uncles, etc., extending only one or two generations past the living. Related patrilines recognize common descent by virtue of membership in the same clan or subclan, though actual genealogical connections are often not remembered.

6 For comparison, consider adjacent or nearby residential blocks in our own society. Individuals and families living on different blocks may interact quite regularly, but not by virtue of their block affiliations. Blocks, in other words, like Ilahita hamlets, do not interact *as such*.

7 This last point bears on a general principle of *regional* cultural convergence, one that resembles the statistical phenomenon known as "regression to the mean." In this instance, through the process of groups on the ground constantly adjusting themselves to each other in accord with their mutual interactive practices – both friendly and hostile – entire regions develop and sustain a relatively uniform settlement pattern. In other words, to the extent that autonomous communities regularly interact (e.g. in war, alliance, trade, ritual cooperation, marriage exchange), there would be a tendency to equilibrate many aspects of life, including social structure and settlement size and type. This appears to have happened in the "Abelamization" of the Ilahita Arapesh.

8 Based on a garbled reading of my earlier reports, Filer (1990) challenges my designation of Ilahita as a "village." Among other misapprehensions, he describes me as justifying this treatment on the grounds that the community is residentially contiguous and is a defensive unit. While these features surely describe Ilahita, they are not why both the residents and I designate it as a *village*; rather, it is due to the fact that the community is bound together by a common, centralized ritual system. Ilahita is explicitly a spiritual whole, created, sustained, and ruled over by the parliament of invisible beings (tambarans) who, together, are the transcendent, capitalized Tambaran. The material to be presented in Chapters 6 and 7 should leave no doubt as to the accuracy of the "village" designation, though it will also be seen that one of the

wards (Ilifalemb) is arguably independent of the other five. The issue is of central importance to this study; for, if Ilahita is *not* a village, then virtually the entire argument presented here, fails.

9 By 1985, one of the external settlements had grown considerably and was close to being politically independent from Ililip, the mother ward. This development was part of the process whereby the cessation of warfare removed the pressures holding Ilahita together, enabling dissident groups to spread into the village's hinterland. This emerging pattern of dispersal also suggests that wards have difficulty staying internally cohesive beyond a size of about 300 inhabitants, which is about the maximum limit that prevails in many areas of New Guinea.

10 One of the marvels of general-purpose money is that it drastically reduces this complexity by enabling dissimilar goods and services to be compared and exchanged.

11 It should be understood that Durkheim's terms refer to ideal types. No society is completely one type or the other, but the scheme is useful in identifying different *dimensions* of integration and relative emphases that constitute real and consequential differences between societies.

12 In modern society, gift exchange continues among friends and family; consider, for example, the moral and socially salient aspects of giving and receiving dinner-party invitations, and the exchange of favors of all kinds. Commodity exchange is predominant in the public sphere, the mass scale of which is itself a diagnostic feature of modern society.

6 The dual organization

1 After the French, *moitié*, meaning "half" – the idea being that two halves make a whole.

2 Something approximating this happens in United States national politics. For all intents and purposes, there are only two parties ("moieties"): Democrats (A) and Republicans (B). Each party contains both Liberals (1) and Conservatives (2) (also "moieties"), however, and on some issues ideological position overrides party loyalty. That is to say, some issues unite Liberals against Conservatives, regardless of party. We observe, then, that party moieties cut across ideological moieties, creating a four-square set of possibilities: Democrat-Liberal (A_1), Democrat-Conservative (A_2), Republican-Liberal (B_1), and Republican-Conservative (B_2).

3 This would be as if each of the four political groupings described in note 2 were to be divided into equal numbers of women (x) and men (y), creating an *eight*-square set of possibilities (A_1x, A_1y, A_2x, etc.). These "sex moieties" would cut across *both* party moieties and ideological moieties, and this structure would be activated on issues that place all women in opposition to all men, regardless of party or political philosophy.

4 In previous works dealing with Ilahita social organization (principally, Tuzin 1976, 1980, 1989), these three structures were termed "moieties," "sub-moieties," and "initiation classes." While the previous terminology captured the structurally "nested" character of the multiple dual oppositions, it regrettably obscured their important crosscutting features.

5 For example, cult statues are commissioned by subclans, whereas cult paintings are prepared by individuals. Both types of artistic paraphernalia are transferred

15 Recall that a teleological process is one propelled by an ultimate cause, design, intelligence, or goal. Evolution is *not* teleological, though frequently it appears to be so.

16 In the preceding chapter I described how, within the village-moiety opposition, there is a particular opposition between like ward moieties of "enemy" wards. These ward-moiety competitions are further specified to particular initiation partnerships *vis-à-vis* their Tambaran spirits, which are regarded as mutual enemies (*nautamana*) in the supernatural sphere.

17 Note that A's strategy depends on his understanding of the particular relationship between C and D. If their relations are currently at an ebb, D may well refuse to accept the yam from C, for he is not obliged to take it. C would then face the difficulty of finding another Owapwas man willing to accept the yam, for it would be humiliating for him (and his immediate Sahopwas colleagues) to eat it himself. Figure 5 presupposes that relations between the initiation partners are good and that D accepts the yam. If the relations were known to be strained, A would have arranged for E to be the middleman, by which means D would receive the tuber directly. In this case D would face the prospect of having to eat the yam himself, especially insofar as he is currently not getting along well with C.

18 In its integrative effects this structural innovation in Ilahita is reminiscent of the social reforms instituted by Cleisthenes in late sixth-century Athens. Nisbet (1973: 28–34) describes how the four ancient tribes were abolished and replaced by ten new "tribes", each comprised of ten neighborhood "demes." The crosscutting advantage was achieved by having the constituent demes of each tribe *distributed* across the city, thus discouraging the formation of tribal autonomies that could undermine the overall unity of the city. By Nisbet's reckoning, this new organization enabled Athens to defeat the Persians at Marathon (490 BC) – a victory that inaugurated the "golden age" of classical Athens.

8 Conclusion

1 Interestingly, Blanton *et al.* (1999) posit a similar discontinuity in the events leading up to the rise of the Zapotec state centered at Monte Alban in Oaxaca, southern Mexico. The authors interpret the early San José phase to have been organized on the basis of "a moiety system and public ritual": (p. 130) – institutions that were *not* precursors to state formation at Monte Alban. The actual antecedent conditions, including "the possible development of a chiefdom" (pp. 130–1), "appeared well after the San José phase" (p. 130). Just how the chiefdom itself arose from a pre-existing moiety system or other egalitarian arrangement, the authors do not speculate.

Glossary

Afa'afa'w Senior ward-moiety status, meaning "those who go first." Cf. Ondondof.

Agnates Persons (male or female) related to each other through males.

Balanga One of the six wards of Ilahita; 1970 population, 309.

Bwi'ingili One of the six wards of Ilahita; 1970 population, 172.

Commodity exchange Instrumental, practical, unlike exchange of objects of value, often on a cash basis, in which the parties to the exchange need not have any sort of relationship outside of the transaction. This form of exchange is usually associated with large-scale societies. Cf. Gift exchange.

Dual organization A social system based on structures that are related to each other as binary opposites, usually engaged in reciprocal exchange.

Dual structures The binary categories comprising the dual organization; also called "moieties."

Endogamy Marriage to persons inside the "group," however defined. Cf. Exogamy.

Exogamy Marriage to persons outside the "group," however defined. Cf. Endogamy.

Falanga First and lowest grade of the Tambaran cult, entered at about the age of 5.

Gift exchange Morally embued exchange of objects and services of value, largely done for the purpose of maintaining the multiplex relationship of the parties to the transaction. Frequently assuming a like-for-like form, gift exchange is usually associated with small-scale societies, or small-scale enclaves within large-scale societies. Cf. Commodity exchange.

Hamlet In Ilahita, the smallest named residential unit, usually consisting of a circle of yam and dwelling houses facing on to a clearing, and occupied by one or two patrilines.

Hengwanif One of the six wards of Ilahita; 1970 population, 148.

Ilifalemb One of the six wards of Ilahita; 1970 population, 213.

Ililip One of the six wards of Ilahita; 1970 population, 487.

Initiation moieties Dual structures that are the aggregates of initiation partnerships operating between complementary subclans. Generically, initiation moieties are named Sahopwas ("elder brothers") and Owapwas ("younger brothers"); in this aspect, they, like the ward moieties, cut across the entire society of the village.

Initiation partnerships Hereditary exchange relationships occurring between individuals or agnatic groups belonging to opposite subclans. In aggregate, these partnerships comprise the dualistically opposed initiation moieties, at the village level. Initiation partners exchange initiation goods and services, primarily feast foods, ritual paraphernalia, and ritual instruction.

Initiation submoieties Dual generation division within the initiation moieties, comprised of senior ("father") and junior ("son") statuses.

Lefin Second grade of the Tambaran cult, entered at about the age of 10.

Maolimu Third grade of the Tambaran cult, entered at about the age of 16.

Mechanical social solidarity A form or aspect of society based on a relative lack of differentiation among roles, occupations, and statuses. The integration of groups in such systems is usually based on reciprocal exchange and the giving of like for like. This form of solidarity is usually associated with gift exchange and egalitarianism. Cf. Organic social solidarity.

Moiety One party in a two-party relationship. The Ilahita dual organization is composed of eight interlocking moiety systems. As such, it is the most elaborate instance of dual organization ever documented.

Multiplex relationships Multi-dimensional relationships that are usually embued with moral obligations and expectations, and are usually associated with face-to-face communities and gift exchange. Cf. Simplex relationships.

Nangup One of the six wards of Ilahita; 1970 population, 161.

Nggwal Bunafunei Fourth of five grades of the Tambaran cult, entered into between approximately ages 20 and 45.

Nggwal Walipeine Fifth and highest of five grades of the Tambaran cult, entered into at about the age of 45.

Ondondof Junior ward-moiety status, meaning "those who come behind." Cf. Afa'afa'w.

Organic social solidarity A form or aspect of society based on a relatively differentiated array of roles, occupations, and statuses. The integration of groups in such systems is usually based on the exchange of unlike goods and services. This form of solidarity is usually associated with commodity exchange and hierarchy. Cf. Mechanical social solidarity.

Owapwas Junior ("younger brother") initiation-moiety status. Cf. Sahopwas.

Patriline A group of at least three adjacent generations linked through males. The term implies that this group is less formally constituted and less enduring than a "patrilineage."

Patriliny An ideology according to which descent is reckoned through male links. This ideology may or may not be embodied in formal descent groups (patrilineages or patriclans).

Sahopwas Senior ("older brother") initiation-moiety status. Cf. Owapwas.

Simplex relationships Single-dimension relationships that are usually impersonal and associated with cash and commodity exchange. Cf. Multiplex relationships.

Tambaran Melanesian Pidgin term referring, in the Ilahita case, to the religious ideology, practices, technology, and personifications of the secret men's cults, and synonymous with Tradition.

Ward In Ilahita, one of the six major residential precincts of the village. In residence terms, wards are composed of hamlets; in descent terms, they are composed of clans; in ritual terms, they are composed of two "ward moieties."

Ward moieties A dual structure located within each ward. In this aspect, ward moieties have specific names. Generically, ward moieties are named Afa'afa'w and Ondondof, and in this aspect they, like the initiation moieties, cut across the entire society of the village.

References

Bateson, Gregory 1936. *Naven*. London: Cambridge University Press.

Bateson, Gregory 1972. *Steps to an Ecology of Mind*. New York: Ballantine Books.

Blanton, Richard E., Gary M. Feinman, Stephen A. Kowalewski, and Linda M. Nicholas 1999. *Ancient Oaxaca*. Cambridge: Cambridge University Press.

Boas, Franz 1896. The Limitations of the Comparative Method of Anthropology. *Science* 4: 901–8.

Bowlby, John 1971. *Attachment*. Harmondsworth: Penguin.

Burton, Maurice, and Robert Burton 1969. "Cassowary." *The International Wildlife Encyclopedia*, vol. 3. New York: Marshall Cavendish.

Carneiro, Robert L. 1970. A Theory of the Origin of the State. *Science* 169: 733–8.

Carneiro, Robert L. 1981. "The Chiefdom: Precursor of the State." In Grant D. Jones and Robert R. Kautz, eds, *The Transition to Statehood in the New World*. New York: Cambridge University Press, pp. 37–79.

Carneiro, Robert L. 1991. "The Nature of the Chiefdom as Revealed by Evidence from the Cauca Valley of Colombia." In A. Terry Rambo and Kathleen Gillogly, eds, *Profiles in Cultural Evolution*. Ann Arbor: Museum of Anthropology, University of Michigan, pp. 167–90.

Childe, V. Gordon 1950. The Urban Revolution. *The Town Planning Review* 21: 3–17.

Cohen, Ronald, and Elman R. Service, eds, 1978. *Origins of the State: The Anthropology of Political Evolution*. Philadelphia: Institute for the Study of Human Issues.

Diamond, Jared 1997. *Guns, Germs, and Steel: The Fates of Human Societies*. New York: W.W. Norton.

Durkheim, Emile 1933 (orig. 1893). *Division of Labor in Society*, trans. G. Simpson. New York: Macmillan.

Eggan, Fred 1937. Historical Changes in the Choctaw Kinship System. *American Anthropologist* 39: 34–52.

Eggan, Fred 1950. *Social Organization of the Western Pueblos*. Chicago: University of Chicago Press.

Feil, D.K. 1987. *The Evolution of Highland Papua New Guinea Societies*. Cambridge: Cambridge University Press.

Filer, Colin 1990. "Diversity of Cultures or Culture of Diversity?" In N. Lutkehaus, C. Kaufmann, W.E. Mitchell, D. Newton, L. Osmundsen, and M. Schuster, eds, *Sepik Heritage: Tradition and Change in Papua New Guinea*. Durham: Carolina Academic Press, pp. 116–28.

Flannery, Kent V. 1968. "Archeological Systems Theory and Early Mesoamerica." In B.J. Meggers, ed., *Anthropological Archaeology in the Americas*. Washington, DC: Anthropological Society of Washington, pp. 67–87.

Flannery, Kent V. 1994. "Childe the Evolutionist: A Perspective from Nuclear America." In David R. Harris, ed., *The Archaeology of V. Gordon Childe*. Chicago: University of Chicago Press, pp. 101–19.

Flannery, Kent V. 1999. Process and Agency in Early State Formation. *Cambridge Archaeological Journal* 9(1): 3–21.

Forge, Anthony 1966. Art and Environment in the Sepik. *Proceedings of the Royal Anthropological Institute, 1965*, pp. 23–31.

Forge, Anthony 1972a. "Normative Factors in the Settlement Size of Neolithic Cultivators (New Guinea)." In Peter J. Ucko, Ruth Tringham, and G.W. Dimbleby, eds, *Man, Settlement and Urbanism*. London: Duckworth, pp. 363–76.

Forge, Anthony 1972b. The Golden Fleece. *Man* 7: 527–40.

Forge, Anthony 1990. "The Power of Culture and the Culture of Power." In N. Lutkehaus, C. Kaufmann, W.E. Mitchell, D. Newton, L. Osmundsen, and M. Schuster, eds, *Sepik Heritage: Tradition and Change in Papua New Guinea*. Durham: Carolina Academic Press, pp. 160–70.

Fortes, Meyer 1969. *Kinship and the Social Order: The Legacy of Lewis Henry Morgan*. Chicago: Aldine Press.

Fortune, Reo 1939. Arapesh Warfare. *American Anthropologist* 41: 22–41.

Fox, Robin 1967. *The Keresan Bridge: A Problem in Pueblo Ethnology*. London: Athlone Press.

Fried, Morton H. 1967. *The Evolution of Political Society*. New York: Random House.

Glasgow, D., and R. Loving 1964. *Languages of the Maprik Sub-District*. Port Moresby: Department of Information and Extension Services.

Godelier, Maurice 1986. *The Making of Great Men: Male Domination and Power Among the New Guinea Baruya*, trans. R. Swyer. Cambridge: Cambridge University Press.

Godelier, Maurice, and Marilyn Strathern, eds, 1991. *Big Men and Great Men: Personifications of Power in Melanesia*. Cambridge: Cambridge University Press.

Gould, Stephen J., and Niles Eldredge 1977. Punctuated Equilibria: The Tempo and Mode of Evolution Reconsidered. *Palaeontology* 3: 115–51.

Harris, David R., ed. 1994. *The Archaeology of V. Gordon Childe: Contemporary Perspectives*. Chicago: University of Chicago Press.

Harris, Marvin 1977. *Cannibals and Kings: The Origins of Cultures*. New York: Random House.

Harrison, Simon 1993. *The Mask of War: Violence, Ritual and the Self in Melanesia*. Manchester: Manchester University Press.

Hauptmann, Harald 1993. "Ein Kultgebäude in Nevali Çori." In M. Frangipane, H. Hauptmann, M. Liverani, P. Matthiae, and M. Mellink, eds, *Between the*

Rivers and Over the Mountains: Archaeologica Anatolica et Mesopotamica Alba Palmieri Dedicata. Rome: Università di Roma, pp. 37–69.

Hauptmann, Harald 1999. "The Urfa Region." In Mehmet Ozdogan and Nezih Basgelen, eds, Neolithic in Turkey: The Cradle of Civilization. Istanbul: Arkeoloji Ve Sanat Yayinlari, pp. 65–86.

Hogbin, H. Ian, and Camilla Wedgwood 1953/4. Local Grouping in Melanesia. Oceania 33(4): 241–76, 34(1): 58–76.

Hope, Geoff, and Jack Golson 1995. Late Quaternary change in the mountains of New Guinea. Antiquity 69(265): 818–30.

James, William 1911. "The Moral Equivalent of War." In W. James, Memories and Studies. London: Longmans, Green, pp. 265–96.

Johnson, Allen W., and Timothy Earle 1987. The Evolution of Human Societies: From Foraging Group to Agrarian State. Stanford: Stanford University Press.

Johnson, Gregory A. 1982. "Organizational Structure and Scalar Stress." In Colin Renfrew, Michael J. Rowlands, and Barbara Abbott Segraves, eds, Theory and Explanation in Archaeology: The Southampton Conference. New York: Academic Press, pp. 389–421.

Lawrence, Peter 1964. Road Belong Cargo: A Study of the Cargo Movement in the Southern Madang District, New Guinea. Manchester: Manchester University Press.

Laycock, Donald C. 1973. Sepik Languages: Checklist and Preliminary Classification. Pacific Linguistics 7(1): 36–66.

Leavitt, Stephen C. 1989. Cargo, Christ, and Nostalgia for the Dead: Themes of Intimacy and Abandonment in Bumbita Arapesh Social Experience. Unpublished Ph.D. dissertation, University of California, San Diego.

Lepervanche, Marie de. 1967/8. Descent, Residence and Leadership in the New Guinea Highlands. Oceania 38(2): 134–58, 38(3): 163–89.

Lévi-Strauss, Claude 1969 (orig. 1949). The Elementary Structures of Kinship. Boston: Beacon Press.

Lewis, Gilbert 1975. Knowledge of Illness in a Sepik Society. London: Athlone Press.

Lindenbaum, Shirley 1987. "The Mystification of Female Labors." In Jane Collier and Sylvia Yanagisako, eds, Gender and Kinship: Essays Toward a Unified Analysis. Stanford: Stanford University Press, pp. 221–43.

Marcus, Joyce, and Kent V. Flannery 1996. Zapotec Civilization: How Urban Society Evolved in Mexico's Oaxaca Valley. London: Thames and Hudson.

Mauss, Marcel 1967 (orig. 1925). The Gift: Forms and Functions of Exchange in Archaic Societies. New York: W.W. Norton.

Maybury-Lewis, David, and Uri Almagor, eds, 1989. The Attraction of Opposites: Thought and Society in the Dualistic Mode. Ann Arbor: University of Michigan Press.

McCarthy, J.K. 1963. Patrol into Yesterday: My New Guinea Years. Melbourne: F.W. Cheshire.

Mead, Margaret 1935. Sex and Temperament in Three Primitive Societies. London: Routledge.

Mead, Margaret 1938. The Mountain Arapesh: An Importing Culture. American Museum of Natural History, Anthropological Papers 37(3): 319–451.

150 References

Mead, Margaret 1947. The Mountain Arapesh: Socio-Economic Life. American Museum of Natural History, *Anthropological Papers* 40(3): 163–232.

Mitchell, William E. 1978. *The Bamboo Fire: An Anthropologist in New Guinea.* New York: Norton.

Morgan, Lewis Henry 1877. *Ancient Society.* New York: Holt.

Nisbet, Robert 1973. *The Social Philosophers: Community & Conflict in Western Thought.* New York: Thomas Y. Crowell.

Parish, Steven M. 1996. *Hierarchy and Its Discontents: Culture and the Politics of Consciousness in Caste Society.* Philadelphia: University of Pennsylvania Press.

Popper, Karl 1950. *The Open Society and Its Enemies,* vol. 2. Princeton: Princeton University Press.

Radcliffe-Brown, A.R. 1952 (orig. 1940). "On Social Structure." In A.R. Radcliffe-Brown, *Structure and Function in Primitive Society.* New York: Free Press, pp. 188–204.

Rand McNally 1999. *Quick Reference World Atlas.* New York: Rand McNally.

Rappaport, Roy A. 1968. *Pigs for the Ancestors: Ritual in the Ecology of a New Guinea People.* New Haven: Yale University Press.

Reiner, E.J., and R.G. Robbins 1964. The Middle Sepik Plains, New Guinea: A Physiographic Study. *Geographical Review* 54(1): 20–44.

Renfrew, Colin, and Paul Bahn 1991. *Archaeology: Theories Methods and Practice.* London: Thames & Hudson.

Rubel, Paula G., and Abraham Rosman 1978. *Your Own Pigs You May Not Eat: A Comparative Study of New Guinea Societies.* Chicago: University of Chicago Press.

Sahlins, Marshall D., and Elman R. Service 1960. *Evolution and Culture.* Ann Arbor: University of Michigan Press.

Sanders, William T., and Joseph Marino 1970. *New World Prehistory: Archaeology of the American Indian.* Englewood Cliffs, NJ: Prentice-Hall.

Sanders, William T., and Barbara J. Price 1968. *Mesoamerica: The Evolution of a Civilization.* New York: Random House.

Schwartz, Theodore 1975. "Cultural Totemism." In George De Vos and Lola Romanucci-Ross, eds, *Ethnic Identity: Cultural Continuities and Change.* Palo Alto CA: Mayfield Publishing Co., pp. 106–32.

Scott, James C. 1998. *Seeing Like a State: How Certain Schemes to Improve the Human Condition Have Failed.* New Haven: Yale University Press.

Service, Elman R. 1971 (orig. 1962). *Primitive Social Organization: An Evolutionary Perspective.* New York: Random House.

Simmel, Georg 1950. "The Secret and the Secret Society." In Kurt H. Wolff, ed. and trans., *The Sociology of Georg Simmel.* New York: Free Press.

Steward, Julian H. 1955. *Theory of Culture Change: The Methodology of Multilinear Evolution.* Urbana: University of Illinois Press.

Tattersall, Ian 1998. *Becoming Human: Evolution and Human Uniqueness.* New York: Harcourt Brace.

Townsend, G.W.L. 1968. *District Officer: From Untamed New Guinea to Lake Success, 1921–46.* Sydney: Pacific Publications.

Trigger, Bruce G. 1998. *Sociocultural Evolution: Calculation and Contingency*. Oxford: Blackwell.

Tuzin, Donald 1972. Yam Symbolism in the Sepik: An Interpretative Account. *Southwestern Journal of Anthropology* 28(3): 230–54.

Tuzin, Donald 1976. *The Ilahita Arapesh: Dimensions of Unity*. Berkeley: University of California Press.

Tuzin, Donald 1980. *The Voice of the Tambaran: Truth and Illusion in Ilahita Arapesh Religion*. Berkeley: University of California Press.

Tuzin, Donald 1982. "Ritual Violence Among the Ilahita Arapesh: The Dynamics of Moral and Religious Uncertainty." In Gilbert H. Herdt, ed., *Rituals of Manhood: Male Initiation in Papua New Guinea*. Berkeley: University of California Press, pp. 321–55.

Tuzin, Donald 1983. "Cannibalism and Arapesh Cosmology: A War-Time Incident with the Japanese." In Paula Brown and Donald Tuzin, eds, *The Ethnography of Cannibalism*. Society for Psychological Anthropology, Special Publication. Washington, DC: Society for Psychological Anthropology, pp. 61–71.

Tuzin, Donald 1989. "The Organization of Action, Identity, and Experience in Arapesh Dualism." In David Maybury-Lewis and Uri Almagor, eds, *The Attraction of Opposites: Thought and Society in the Dualistic Mode*. Ann Arbor: University of Michigan Press, pp. 277–96.

Tuzin, Donald 1991. "The Cryptic Brotherhood of Big Men and Great Men in Ilahita." In Maurice Godelier and Marilyn Strathern, eds, *Big Men and Great Men: Personifications of Power in Melanesia*. Cambridge: Cambridge University Press, pp. 115–29.

Tuzin, Donald 1995. Art and Procreative Illusion in the Sepik: Comparing the Abelam and the Arapesh. *Oceania* 65(4): 289–303.

Tuzin, Donald 1997. *The Cassowary's Revenge: The Life and Death of Masculinity in a New Guinea Society*. Chicago: University of Chicago Press.

Tyler, Edward B. 1871. *Primitive Culture: Researches into the Development of Mythology, Philosophy, Religion, Language, Art and Custom*. London: J. Murray.

Tyler, Edward B. 1889. "On a Method of Investigating the Development of Institutions; Applied to Laws of Marriage and Descent." In Nelson Graburn, ed., *Readings in Kinship and Social Structure*. New York: Harper & Row, 1971, pp. 19–31.

Watson, James B. 1963. A Micro-Evolution Study in New Guinea. *Journal of the Polynesian Society* 72: 188–92.

Weiner, Annette B. 1992. *Inalienable Possessions: The Paradox of Keeping-While-Giving*. Berkeley: University of California Press.

White, Leslie 1959. *The Evolution of Culture*. New York: McGraw-Hill.

White, Leslie 1960. "Preface." In Marshall D. Sahlins and Elman R. Service, *Evolution and Culture*. Ann Arbor: University of Michigan Press, pp. v–xii.

Wittfogel, Karl 1957. *Oriental Despotism*. New Haven: Yale University Press.

Yoffee, Norman 1993. "Too Many Chiefs? (or, Safe Texts for the '90s)." In Norman Yoffee and Andrew Sherratt, eds, *Archaeological Theory: Who Sets the Agenda?* Cambridge: Cambridge University Press, pp. 60–78.

Index

Abelam (cultural group) ix, x, 53–4,
    55, 57, 92, 135nn. 2, 4, 136n. 8;
    effect on Ilahita 15, 17, 56, 58, 61,
    71, 74, 93, 120–2 *passim*, 123, 126,
    135n. 5, 136n. 6, 136n. 7, 137n. 7,
    139n. 11
adaptation 54–5, 69, 84; agricultural
    21, 28, 37; social 4, 9, 65, 120–2,
    125, 129
adoption 69, 109–11, 140n. 11; case of
    111–4; *see also* kinship
Afa'afa'w *see* moieties, ward
age: and ritual rank 9, 95, 96
aggression 66–7, 71, 74, 84, 98, 139n.
    2; sublimated 109, 113, 118–9;
    veiled 115–8; *see also*
    competition
Allen, B.J. 134n. 20
Almagor, U. 10
ancestors 31, 34, 62, 63, 92, 96, 101,
    128, 136n. 6, 140n. 45; *see also*
    descent; spirits
archaeology 5, 7, 8, 52, 125
art: as a feature of the Tambaran ix, x,
    22, 43, 55, 77, 92–3, 121, 138n. 5
artists 9, 33–4, 138n. 5
Athens (Greece) 141n. 18
Atitapwin (case) 111–4, 140n. 14
Australian Aborigines 10
Australian rule; *see* colonial era;
    modernization; World War II
authority, ritual; *see* elders, ritual;
    Nggwal Walipeine; Tambaran

Bahn, P. 7

Balanga (ward) 72, 73, 74, 82, 84, 87,
    94, 117–8, 139n. 6
Bandangel; *see* moieties, village
band-level societies 6, 7, 9; *see also*
    types, societal
Bateson, G. x, 136n. 6
big man (leadership form) 8, 20, 67,
    68
Blanton, R.E. 7, 141n. 1
Boas, F. 2, 130n. 1
body 33–7 *passim*, 39, 62, 63, 99, 100,
    102, 103, 105–6, 113, 133n. 18,
    134n. 21, 140nn. 5, 7; *see also* food
Boiken (cultural group) 135n. 5
Bowlby, J. 120
brideprice 48, 135n. 10
Bumbita Arapesh (cultural group) 54
Bwi'ingili (ward) 73, 74, 82, 84, 90, 94,
    139n. 6

camps, residential 16, 42, 71, 101
cargo cults 44–5
Carneiro, R. 121, 130n. 2, 131n. 4,
    136n. 10
cash crops 17, 24, 46–7, 68, 132n. 5
cash 17, 45–8, 49, 123, 127, 132n. 6,
    133n. 9, 138n. 10
Cassowary-Mother, *see*
    "Nambweapa'w"
Chambri (cultural group) x
change: as incessant in society 4, 123;
    mechanisms of 5, 7, 8, 9, 83–4,
    121–2, 124–9; potential for 8–9,
    126, 128–9, 131n. 6, 141n. 1; *see
    also* colonial era, cultural contact;

elders, ritual, threats to authority of;
modernization; social evolution;
warfare, cessation of
chiefdoms 6, 7, 8, 9, 21, 68, 130nn. 2,
3, 141n. 1; *see also* types, societal
Childe, V.G. 5, 125
Christianity; *see* mission; Revival
clans 55, 56, 74, 80–9 *passim*, 101, 103,
112–3, 125, 128, 136n. 6, 137n. 5,
139n. 2; *see also* descent groups
Clarke, W.C. 23
Cleisthenes 141n. 18
Cohen, R. 131n. 4
collectivism; *see* individualism
colonial era ix, 3, 9, 14, 15, 16–7, 18,
19, 22, 40–51, 72, 121, 123, 134nn.
1, 2, 136n. 9
competition 34, 43, 46, 78, 84, 113,
127, 141nn. 16, 17; *see also*
aggression; fraternal rivalry
conflict; *see* disputes
contact; *see* cultural contact
cosmology 15, 38–9
council, local government 48–9
courts, village 16, 17, 49–51, 123
cultural contact 3, 15, 16, 17, 38–46,
53–4, 55–6, 121, 123, 134n. 1,
136n. 9; *see also* colonial era;
cultural self-objectification
cultural self-objectification 15, 38, 44,
121, 126, 134n. 6

Darwin, C. 7
death 37, 39, 40, 60, 63, 100–3, *passim*,
133n. 17, 139n. 3, 140nn. 5, 7; *see
also* mortuary rites; Tambaran, and
death
deception; *see* female; "Nambweapa'w"
demography 35–6; effects on dual
organization of 18, 94–5, 107–8,
122, 125, 128; *see also* death;
population
descent groups 18, 37, 49, 55, 68, 74,
80, 80–1, 82, 83, 85, 88–9, 90, 113,
125, 137n. 5
descent 28, 34, 85, 88, 92–3, 107, 113,
120, 127, 139n. 9; *see also*
inheritance; kinship
Diamond, J. 130n. 1, 131n. 4, 132n. 2,
139n. 7

diet; *see* food
disputes 71, 74, 99–100, 102, 105–6,
115–20, 127; *see also* aggression;
courts; Tambaran, as agent of social
control
divination 99–100, 101, 140nn. 5, 7;
see also death; Tambaran, and death
dual organization 10–1, 127; and
ritualized competition 84–7, 87–8,
94, 115–20; as adapted to village
population size 18, 77, 79, 81, 83,
84–5, 94–5, 124–5; as the
infrastructure of the Tambaran 11,
18, 79, 83, 93, 95, 123; cross-cutting
aspects of 78, 80, 81, 87–8, 90–1,
95, 107, 119, 138nn. 2, 3, 141n. 18;
self-regulating aspects of 18, 79,
83–4, 89, 107–9, 110–1, 113–5,
124, 140n. 10; spatial aspects of 81,
84, 87, 88–9, 119; structures of 11,
78–94, 140n. 8; symbolic features of
78–9, 85–7, 87, 90, 125–6;
uncognized character of 83–4, 109,
114–5; *see also* mechanical
solidarity; moieties
Durkheim, E. 75, 76, 138n. 11

Earle, T. 8, 58, 130n. 1, 131n. 4, 136n.
10
education; *see* schools
egalitarianism 8, 18, 37, 60, 75–6, 127,
128, 141n. 1
Eggan, F. 3
elders, ritual 9, 37, 91, 95, 96, 99–100,
102, 103–4, 121, 128–9, 133n. 18,
139n. 11; threats to authority of 17,
43, 44, 48, 106, 123, 128–9; *see also*
Nggwal Walipeine
Eldredge, N. 131n. 6
evolution; *see* Neo-Evolutionism;
social evolution; Victorian
anthropology
exchange; *see* reciprocity; gift
exchange

Falanga (Tambaran grade) 28–9, 36
family; *see* adoption; kinship; mothers;
sibling relations; socialization
feasting 29, 30, 32, 60, 95, 98, 101,
104

Feil, D., 21, 67, 130n. 1, 132n. 1
female: ritual exclusion 11, 33, 36,
45, 55, 60–1, 64–5, 98, 121,
131n. 8, 133nn. 18, 19,
134nn. 22, 23; symbolism 25–6,
28–9, 131n. 8; see also masculinity;
mothers
femininity; see female
Filer, C. 135n. 1, 137n. 8
Flannery, K.V. 5, 8, 67, 83, 84, 131n.
4, 136n. 10
food 24–9 passim, 30, 35–6, 46, 62, 63,
94, 132nn. 6, 7, 133nn. 9, 16, 18,
19; see also feasting; gardening;
hunting; sago; yams;
Forge, A. x–xi, 1, 54, 56, 67, 127,
136n. 8, 139n. 11
Fortes, M. 67
Fortune, R. x, 135n. 5
Fox, R. 3
fraternal rivalry 70–71, 109, 113, 119,
120, 134n. 21; see also aggression;
competition; sibling relations
Freeman, D. xi
Fried, M.J. 131n. 4
funeral rites; see mortuary rites

Gaiapo 102
gardening 21–2, 22–4, 30, 31, 33, 36,
37, 46, 68–9, 132nn. 2, 4, 6, 137n.
4
gender 25–6, 28–9, 29–33, 34–5, 35–7,
55, 60, 87, 102, 131n. 8, 133n. 15,
137n. 4; ritual reversal of 12–3; see
also female; masculinity; sexual
division of labor
genital mutilation 29, 62, 131n. 8
geography 17, 18, 19–22, 37, 38, 88,
132n. 2; see also dual organization,
spatial aspects of
ghosts 39, 60, 133n. 17
gift exchange 28, 29, 37, 57, 77, 127,
138n. 12, 139n. 1; see also
reciprocity; mechanical social
solidarity
Glasgow, D. 53
Godelier, M. 21
Golson, J. 20
Gough, C. 40
Gould, S.J. 131n. 6

great man (leadership form) 21, 112–3,
140n. 13

hamlets (residence structures) 68–72,
88; and village integrity 70–1; social
composition of 68–9, 71
Harris, D.R. 131n. 4
Harris, M. 58, 125, 131n. 4, 136n. 10
Harrison, S. 65, 67, 74, 99, 118
Hauptmann, H. 125
Hengwanif (ward) 73, 74, 82, 84, 85,
94, 107, 139n. 6
Heraclitus 123
hereditary transmission: of political
standing 8, 9, 21, 67; of property 28,
29, 88; of initiation partnerships
90–1, 94, 98; see also chiefdoms
hierarchy 8, 37, 75, 127–8; ritually
based 18, 90–1, 103–4, 128–9
highlands; see New Guinea highlands
history 9–10, 16–7, 38–51, 53–4, 56–8,
90, 93, 120–2, 126–7, 128–9, 132n.
2, 136n. 9; anthropological neglect
of 1, 9–10; in British social
anthropology 3–4; see also
prehistory
Hogbin, H.I. 67
Hope, G. 20
horticulture; see gardening; slash-and-
burn horticulture; technology
hunting 24–5, 54, 67, 78, 88–9, 98,
136n. 9, 137n. 4
hunting-gathering subsistence 6, 53,
67; see also hunting; band-level
societies

Iatmul (cultural group) x, 54, 136n. 6
identity; see cultural
self-objectification; gender;
individualism; masculinity
Ilahita Arapesh (cultural group) 22, 54,
56, 62, 70, 74, 115, 135n. 5
Ilahita village ix, 37, 81, 119, 137n. 8;
as ritually sanctified 80, 93, 103–4,
137n. 8; expansion of 1, 10, 17, 56,
58, 71, 120, 121, 122, 123, 124–5,
128; in comparative perspective xi,
52, 56, 58, 66–8, 70, 71–2, 75, 77,
94–5, 97, 100, 104, 124–5, 127–8,
134n. 6, 136n. 8, 137nn. 1, 6, 139n.

11, 141nn. 18, 1; physical layout of 68, 70, 72, 73, 75, 121–2; unusual size of xi, xi–xii, 37, 66–8, 123
Ilifalemb (ward) 73, 74, 81, 82, 85, 137n. 8, 139n. 8
Ililip (ward) 72, 73, 74, 82, 84, 85, 87, 94, 117–8, 139n. 6
imported goods 24, 42, 56, 132nn. 6, 8, 139n. 11; *see also* Abelam (cultural group)
Imul (case) 102–3
incest 76
individualism 46–7, 48, 49–51, 126–7
inheritance 28, 29, 34, 67, 109, 111, 113; *see also* hereditary transmission
initiation moieties; *see* moieties, initiation
initiation partnerships; *see* partnerships, initiation
initiation 28–9, 36, 48, 55, 57, 77, 136n. 6, 138n. 5, 139n. 3, 140n. 14; structures of, 9, 90–1; *see also* moieties, initiation; partnerships, initiation
Inuit (cultural group) 6

James, W. 65
Japanese 40–1, 121, 124, 132n. 6
Johnson, A.W. 8, 58, 130n. 1, 131n. 4, 136n. 10
Johnson, G.A. 79, 127

Kaberry, P. ix–x
kinship 26, 28, 29, 60, 62–3, 68, 93, 98, 101, 102, 103, 110, 118, 136n. 6, 137n. 5, 140n. 14; as a basis of social integration 6, 8, 37, 51, 55, 67, 109, 120, 125, 127, 137n. 3, 139nn. 1, 2; *see also* adoption; fraternal rivalry; marriage; mechanical social solidarity
Kotawa (case) 50
Kowala (case) 102
Ku'umbwili (case) 102–3
Kunai (councilor) 49, 111–4, 140n. 14
Kwanga (cultural group) 56

language 11, 14–5, 20, 38–9, 41, 48, 52–3, 56–8, 63, 74, 131–2n. 9, 132n. 3, 134n. 6, 135n. 1, 136n. 6

Laongol; *see* moieties, village
Laufer, B. 130n. 1
Lawrence, P. 45
Laycock, D.C. 41
Leavitt, S.C. 54
Lefin (Tambaran grade) 28–9, 36, 131n. 8, 134n. 22
Leitipen (case) 101–2
Lepervanche, M. de 1, 67
Lévi-Strauss, C. 76
Lewis, G. 54
Lindenbaum, S. 35
Loving, R. 53

MacArthur, Gen. D. 40
Maolimu (Tambaran grade) 36
Marcus, J. 8, 67, 84
Marino, J. 131n. 4
marriage 55, 60, 62–3, 68, 71, 79–80, 109, 110, 111, 134n. 5, 135n. 10; as basis for social integration 8, 10, 71, 74, 126; sister-exchange 48, 69, 109, 110, 114, 127, 135n. 9
Marx, K. 58
masculinity 23, 34–5, 55–6, 60–1, 64, 115, 121, 123, 137n. 4, 139n. 2
master artists; *see* artists
Mauss, M. 77
Maybury-Lewis, D. 10
McCarthy, J.K. 134n. 1
Mead, M. x, 54, 55–6, 60, 135nn. 2, 3
mechanical social solidarity 10, 18, 28, 75–7, 79, 84, 100, 120–1, 126, 127; limits of, 10, 126, 128–9; *see also* dual organization; reciprocity
Melanesian Pidgin 14–5, 48, 131n. 9
men's cult; *see* Tambaran
methodology 5, 6–9, 17–8, 52–3, 66, 97, 123, 130–1n. 3, 131n. 4, 138n. 11; *see also* typological analysis
misogyny; *see* female; masculinity
mission 42–5, 121, 123, 132n. 6, 134n. 4
Mitchell, W.E. 54
modernization 15–6, 17, 45–51, 121–2, 126–7, 133n. 9, 138n. 12
moieties 78, 138nn. 1, 2, 3, 4, 140n. 8; initiation 80, 81–2, 90–1, 108, 114, 140n. 9, 141nn. 17, 1; initiation sub- 108, 114, 139n. 10; village 80,

81–2, 84–7, 92, 108. 116–7, 141n.
16; ward 80, 81–2, 87–90, 92, 95,
108, 115, 116–8, 119, 141n. 16; *see
also* dual organization
Moluccas (archipelago) 136n. 9
Monte Alban (Mexico) 141n. 1
moral dilemma 17, 60–2, 64–5, 98,
136n. 9
Morgan, L.H. 1
mortuary rites 29, 60, 84
mothers 29, 35–6, 44, 62–3, 133n. 17;
see also female symbolism; kinship;
socialization
Mountain Arapesh (cultural group) x,
xi, 53, 54, 55–6, 60, 70, 135nn. 2, 3,
5
Mundugumor (cultural group) x
mythology 25, 52, 61–4, 133n. 17,
136n. 9, 139n. 9

"Nambweapa'w" (myth) 62–3, 96,
136n. 9, 139n. 9
Nangup (ward) 73, 74, 81, 82, 84
Neo-Evolutionism 127, 130n. 1, 130n.
3
Neo-Melanesian; *see* Melanesian
Pidgin
New Guinea highlands x, 20–2, 34,
132n. 1
Nggwal Bunafunei (Tambaran grade)
12, 13, 37, 57, 80, 90, 91, 104, 112,
121
Nggwal Walipeine (Tambaran grade)
37, 80, 91, 95, 96, 104, 121, 128–9;
see also elders, ritual; hierarchy;
Tambaran, grades of
Nisbet, R. 141n. 18

Ondondof; *see* moieties, ward
organic model of society 3–4
organic social solidarity 28, 74, 79, 126,
127–8
Owapwas; *see* moieties, initiation

Papua New Guinea 15–6, 19, 48–9,
123, 127, 134n. 2, 140n. 6
Parish, S. 128
partnerships, initiation 80, 90–1, 94,
98, 102–3, 107, 111, 141nn. 16, 17;
secondary 94, 107

pigs 20, 34, 36–7, 76, 78, 88–9, 98,
104, 132n. 1, 133n. 10; as
"children" 24, 28, 88–9, 133n. 10
Popper, K. 83–4, 139n. 7
population 22; and societal complexity
6, 10, 24, 58, 65, 66, 68, 77, 79, 81,
89, 94–5, 120–1, 123–5, 126; and
subsistence 5, 44; movements 53–4,
56–8, 71, 74, 79, 81, 84–5, 89, 100,
120, 121, 122, 135nn. 3, 4, 5, 137n.
2, 138n. 9; *see also* demography;
social evolution
prehistory 16, 52–6, 71, 125, 126,
132n. 2, 136n. 6; difficulties of
inquiring into, 2–3, 52, 130n. 3,
135nn. 2, 3, 4, 5, 139n. 2
Price, B.J. 131n. 4
Prince Alexander mountains 21, 40,
134n. 2, 135n. 2
property tenure 23, 28, 46–7, 52, 68,
77, 109, 111, 126; *see also* descent
groups; individualism
"punctuated equilibria" 131n. 6, 136n.
10

Radcliffe-Brown, A.R. 3, 4
rank; *see* hierarchy
Rappaport, R.A. 105, 127
reciprocity 10, 28, 29, 51, 69, 76, 77,
79, 84, 90–1, 94, 99, 106, 107, 109;
see also competition; gift exchange;
mechanical social solidarity
refugees; *see* population, movements
Reiner, E.J. 135n. 4
Renfrew, C. 7
residence: patterns 18, 68–9; structures
68–72, 72–5; units, cohesion of 67,
70–1, 75, 76, 118–20, 138n. 9,
139n. 2
Revival (religious movement) 45, 48,
64, 133n. 10
Robbins, R.G. 135n. 4
Roscoe, P. 135n. 5
Rosman, A. 76
Rubel, P. 76

sacrifice, human; *see* Tambaran, and
death
sago 21, 25–9, 55; maternal symbolism
of 25–6, 28–9; processing 26–8

158 *Index*

Sahlins, M. 131n. 4
Sahopwas; *see* moieties, initiation
San (cultural group) 6
Sanders, W.T. 131n. 4
schools 16, 17, 47–8
Schrader, L. 134n. 4
Schwartz, T. 134n. 6
Scott, J.C. 139n. 7
secrecy, ritual; *see* female
segmentary societies 6, 7, 9, 75–6, 109,
  130n. 2; *see also* types, societal
Sepik river (cultural region) 21, 38, 53,
  55, 74, 134–5n. 7
Service, E.R. 2, 130n. 2, 131n. 4
settlements: limitations of size of in
  New Guinea xi, 67, 54, 67, 70;
  patterns 20–1, 23–4, 42, 54–5, 67,
  70, 137n. 7, 139n. 2
sexual division of labor 21–2, 26, 34–5,
  36, 37, 46, 62
sharing ethic 6, 28, 37, 69, 137n. 3; *see
  also* egalitarianism
sibling relations 29, 36, 62–3, 70–1, 74,
  92, 134n. 21; *see also* fraternal
  rivalry
Simmel, G. 61
sister-exchange marriage; *see* marriage,
  sister-exchange
slash-and-burn horticulture 23, 37, 46,
  67, 135n. 4
social complexity, emergence of; *see*
  social evolution
social control; *see* Tambaran, as agent
  of social control
social evolution 7–8, 65, 66–7, 83–4,
  123, 124, 125, 127–8, 130n. 3,
  131nn. 4, 5, 6, 132n. 1, 139n. 7,
  141n. 18; in Ilahita 37, 58, 65, 77,
  79–80, 90, 94–5, 103–4, 114–5,
  120–2, 123–9; anthropological
  neglect of 1, 9–10; in American
  cultural anthropology 3, 130n. 1; in
  British social anthropology 4; in
  Ilahita 17, 18, 22, 54
socialization 28–9, 35–7, 48
Songwanda'a (case) 102
sorcery 45, 67, 98, 100–1, 113, 117–8,
  127, 140nn. 4, 5, 6; cases of 101–3
South Sea Evangelical Mission
  (SSEM); *see* mission

spirit house ix, 79, 80, 88, 91, 92, 99,
  104, 105, 106, 121
spirits 25, 29–31, 33–4, 55, 77, 80, 92,
  101, 105, 112, 128, 136n. 6, 138n.
  5, 140n. 5, 141n. 16
states 6, 9, 130n. 3; formation of 5,
  125, 127–8; *see also* types, societal
Steward, J. 7, 131n. 4
Strathern, M. 21
structural-functionalism 3–4, 5
subclans 81, 82, 90, 92, 137n. 5, 138n.
  5
subsistence; *see* food
surplus resources 8, 34, 58
Swan Maiden; *see* "Nambweapa'w"
sweet potato 20, 34, 132nn. 1, 6
swidden horticulture; *see* slash-and-
  burn horticulture

Tambaran (men's cult) 11–7, 37, 43,
  47–8, 60, 65, 76, 77, 92–3, 120,
  121, 126, 128–9, 139nn. 11, 2, 3,
  141n. 16; and death 99–100, 101–3,
  139n. 3; and war 11, 45, 55, 57,
  98–9, 121, 139n. 3; as adopted from
  Abelam 15, 56, 58, 60; as agent of
  social control 43, 45, 95, 99–100,
  101–7, 140n. 4; as icon of Tradition
  and village spiritual unity 14, 15,
  16, 24, 44, 80, 83, 93, 103, 104–7,
  128, 137n. 8; death of 16, 17, 44,
  45, 48, 64–5, 98, 123, 126, 129,
  135n. 8; ethical features of 99–100,
  101–7, 121, 129; grades of 8–9, 11,
  28–9, 36–7, 88, 90–1, 95, 98, 112,
  121, 128–9, 134n. 22; magical work
  of 11, 29, 43, 83, 88–9, 91, 98, 105;
  paraphernalia of 11, 13, 14, 22, 77,
  80, 91, 92, 93, 95, 96, 134n. 22,
  138n. 5. *See also* Falanga;
  initiation; Lefin; Maolimu; Nggwal
  Bunafunei; Nggwal Walipeine;
  partnerships, initiation; sorcery;
  spirit house
Tattersall, I. 127, 131nn. 5, 6, 136n. 10
taxonomies; *see* typological analysis
technology 5, 17, 37, 63, 66, 132n. 8,
  133n. 10, 134n. 22; gardening 21–2,
  23, 30, 31, 33, 34–5, 46, 132n. 4,
  133n. 19, 135n. 4; hunting 24–5,

133n. 14; spirit-house 91, 104–5, 106; sago-processing 26–8, 133n. 16
teleology 84, 114–5, 141n. 15
tenure; *see* property tenure
To'ongolal (case) 111–4
Tok Pisin; *see* Melanesian Pidgin
Torricelli mountains 21, 53, 61; *see also* language
totemism 85, 87, 90, 92, 134n. 6, 139n. 9
Townsend, G.W.L. 134n. 1
tribes; *see* segmentary societies
Trigger, B.G. 131n. 4
Tuzin, B. xi, 60
Tuzin, D. 9, 11, 26, 34, 36, 42, 49, 60, 65, 74, 80, 93, 98, 103, 109, 110n, 115, 131nn. 6, 8, 134n. 4, 135n. 8, 136nn. 8, 9, 138n. 4, 139n. 5, 140n. 9
Tyler, E.B. 1, 76
types, societal 6, 67, 124, 125, 126–7, 130n. 2
typological analysis 6–9, 97, 127, 130–1n. 3, 138n. 11

Victorian anthropology 1–2, 127, 130n. 1
village moieties; *see* moieties, village
violence; *see* aggression

Waipisi (case) 111–4, 140n. 13
ward moieties; *see* moieties ward
wards (residence structures) 56, 72–5
warfare 21, 24, 37, 40–2, 53–8 *passim*, 67, 98, 105, 121–2, 135nn. 4, 5, 136n. 7, 136n. 10, 137n. 2; cessation of 15, 16, 22, 42, 65, 70, 71, 100, 103, 120, 121, 123, 128, 138n. 9; as promoting village solidarity 10, 16, 18, 42, 65, 70, 71, 100, 120, 139nn. 2, 3
Watson, J.B. 1
Wedgwood, C. 67
Weiner, A.B. 76
White, L. 5, 130n. 1
Wittfogel, K. 125
women; *see* female; gender; mothers
World War I x, 22
World War II x, 17, 40–2, 71, 81, 121–2, 132n. 6, 134n. 3

yams 29–35, 37, 54, 68, 76, 98, 115, 134n. 20; as artifacts 31, 33; as masculine symbols 23, 34, 133nn. 18, 19, 137n. 4; as objects of competition and exchange 33, 34, 46, 54, 84, 94, 111, 115–8, 141n. 17
Yoffee, N. 7, 125, 130n. 3, 131n. 4